Write Songs from Scratch

Chris Norton

A complete guide to
songwriting for beginners

BOOSEY & HAWKES

London · New York · Berlin · Sydney

Introduction

Write Songs from Scratch is intended for anyone who wants to begin writing songs. It suggests different ways of getting started and contains useful tips about how to write your ideas down. And, using specially-written songs as examples, it shows how you can develop and refine songs into fully professional chart-toppers. There is also some information about how professional songwriters go about getting their work published and some basic advice about legal protection for you and your work.

Write Songs from Scratch assumes you already have some musical knowledge – how to play an instrument, and how to read basic music or chord charts. But you don't need to know about music theory and you will get plenty out of the book and CD even if you can't read music notation.

Contents

Cover design by Electric Echo. Page layout by Anthony Marks.
Printed and bound in England by Halstan & Co. Ltd, Amersham, Bucks.

How the book is organised

Symbols at the side of the pages identify key points, things to do and other helpful signposts through the book.

The symbol on the right identifies an activity which needs a pen and paper. As this book is about writing, you will see this one quite frequently.

From time to time there are suggestions of music to listen to. These are shown by the symbol on the right. All the recommendations are easy to find in a music store or a good library – you may even know some of them already. It's useful to listen to them as they demonstrate important points about songwriting. However, you don't have to listen to these to continue working through the book.

Arrows like the one on the right contain signposts to other parts of the book (a forward arrow means the information is further on in the book – a backward arrow tells you to go back towards the beginning). Words in orange text are explained more fully on the page referred to in the arrow. Although you don't need to follow them immediately, they point out where to find related information. Keep an eye on them as you go through, as they will help you to remember new concepts and to navigate your way around the book.

The symbol on the right points out "bright ideas". These are usually extra hints, exercises and bits of information which could make learning easier and more enjoyable.

There are more listening suggestions and other hints in the margins.

Using the CD

The CD that comes with this book will help you to hear songwriting in action. It provides exciting opportunities to hear actual songs being constructed and gives you a chance to play or sing with a real band and real singers. To get the most out of the book, you need to use the CD in several different ways. Instructions in the text tell you what to do. The symbol in the margin, shown on the right, shows you which track to select for each activity.

Try to resist the temptation to play the CD all the way through immediately, because some of the activities rely on you not having heard a particular track before.

Recording credits:
Boyfriend: lead vocals, Niqi Brown; backing vocals, Ingrid DuMosch; backing arrangement, Roy Johnson.
I can't live without you: lead vocals, Brent Miller; backing vocals, Roy Johnson; backing arrangement, Roy Johnson.
Something to believe in: lead vocals, Rick Lawson; backing arrangement, Frank Mizen.
You take me away: lead vocals, Roy Johnson; backing vocals, Ingrid DuMosch and Roy Johnson.
Baby my heart: lead and backing vocals, Roy Johnson; backing arrangement, Roy Johnson; acoustic guitar, Pete Haslam.
You tear out my heart: lead vocals, Niqi Brown; backing arrangement, Frank Mizen.
Too much fun: lead vocals, Frank Mizen; backing arrangement, Frank Mizen.
Get your groove on: lead and backing vocals, Roy Johnson.

Your favourite songs

Start by writing down your ten favourite songs. Don't take hours over this, just list the ones that first come to mind. Your songs can be from any era and in any style. (It's fine to change your mind about them tomorrow, too!) The idea is to look at your likes and dislikes to give you clues about where to begin writing. If possible, listen to the songs you have chosen.

Use a notebook to keep a list of songs you like – and songs you don't.

Now go through your list and say what you like about each song. Is it the music? The lyrics? The band or singer that performs it? Then ask some more general questions. Are they all in one style? Are they all from one era? Do they have anything in common? If so, you may already be focusing on a particular style of songwriting. This could help you when you start writing your own songs.

Here's my list:

Come together by the Beatles
Candle in the wind by Elton John
Millennium by Robbie Williams
Fields of gold by Sting
Reeling in the years by Steely Dan

On your way down by Little Feat
Living for the city by Stevie Wonder
Get Miles by Gomez
To Zion by Lauryn Hill
I'll see you again by Noël Coward

Like most people, I like songs from many different periods. My list contains a few quite recent songs (Lauryn Hill, Gomez, Robbie Williams), one from the 1960s (the Beatles), four from the 1970s (Stevie Wonder, Steely Dan, Little Feat, Elton John), one from the 1980s (Sting) and one from the 1930s (Noël Coward).

Try listening to some of these songs. Make a note of your reactions to them.

I like each song for different reasons. In *Come together*, I like the bluesy, gritty riff, the strange vocal quality and the stop before the chorus. I like the vivid images in *Candle in the wind* and the fact that it is easy to remember the tune all the way through. I like the quotation from the James Bond music in *Millennium*; it gives it a yearning quality that seems appropriate for an end-of-century song.

We all like different songs for different reasons. By now you should have noticed that you can like the melody in one song, the vocal quality in another, the lyrics in a third. You can't always separate all the features out, but often some of them appeal to you ahead of the others.

Now make a list of some songs you don't like. Then, in the same way as you did above, say what it is that you don't like about each one. Don't just say "I hate that one!". Ask yourself what it is that annoys you. See if the songs you dislike have anything in common.

Now you have built a picture of your musical taste. Remember that it is important to keep listening to lots of music – even music you don't like – because it helps you to learn about songwriting. The more you think about your likes and dislikes, the more informed your songwriting will be.

The songs on the CD

The songs on tracks 1 to 8 of the CD have been specially written and recorded to help you develop your ideas about songwriting. In order to get the best out of them, follow the sequence below.

1) Listen to each song once. Do you react to any of them instantly? If so, do you like or dislike them? Can you rank them in order of preference?

2) Now listen to the songs a few times. Does your order of preference change once you are reasonably familiar with them?

Nobody reacts to songs in the same way. You may love them all. You may not really like any of them. Don't worry about this. The important thing is to listen critically (and to express your feelings about what you hear).

3) Now, as you did on the opposite page, list what you like about each song. Use as much detail as you can. It doesn't matter if you can't use technical words – just describe what you hear. Maybe you like a particular rhythm, or an instrumental sound, or some of the lyrics stand out. Maybe one of the songs reminds you of another song or singer that you like. Write all this down.

4) Next, write down what you don't like about each song. Again, it's important to explain why.

Wait a few hours, or even a day, before you go on to stage 5. You can still carry on reading the book, but you need to give the songs (and your opinions) time to sink in.

5) Do you remember the songs? Can you sing any of them from memory? Maybe one or more have got "stuck" in your brain (either because you like them or you don't!)

Part of a song that sticks in your brain is called a "hook". A bit of the tune, a few words, even a single sound, can be a hook.

6) Listen to the CD again and look at what you wrote in (3) and (4). Have your opinions changed? Change your list if you like.

7) Are there common features about the things you like and dislike in each of the songs? With the songs you like, are there aspects you dislike? And what about the songs you dislike? Can you find parts that you don't mind too much?

Later on in the book, these preferences will help you to decide where to begin with the songwriting process, so keep your list handy. But this exercise should already have shown you a number of things. Firstly, that your opinions change from first hearing because songs can grow on you (or the opposite); secondly, that certain features "feel" more important to you than others; thirdly, that you have a wide range of likes and dislikes; and fourthly, that what you dislike tells you as much about your musical taste as what you like.

Getting going

Pages 6–9 will help you unpick the different parts of a song and begin to focus on what it is you want to write. They also contain hints about deciding where to begin, which may be helpful even if you have already done some songwriting.

Thinking about songs

Most songs have four basic elements – words, tune, chords and rhythm. You may have identified some of these when doing the activities on the previous pages, and these are the first things we will look at. It may help to listen to some of the songs on the CD again and focus on some of these ingredients separately – jotting down some of the lyrics, humming the tune, tapping the rhythm or picking out some of the chords on a guitar or keyboard.

Beyond these basic elements, songs have other ingredients too. For example, very few songs are the same all the way through. Some sections will be louder than others. They may have a different tune or rhythm, or be faster or slower than the rest. These contrasts add to the success of the finished song. Then there is the way the song is recorded – not just the singing, but the choice of instruments and the style of playing. These aspects, known as the arrangement, are looked at later on in the book, but again, you could listen to some of your favourite songs and think about them now.

31

Different styles of song

Then there's the style of a song. Most people like songs in a variety of styles – a big pop ballad here, a country tune there, a hip-hop song, a dance track and so on. Your first task as a songwriter is to imagine your finished song and its market. Do you want to write pop songs for boy- or girl-bands? Or big ballads for someone like Mariah Carey, or country tunes for Shania Twain? Perhaps you want to write a musical, a heavy rock anthem or a smooth soul song. Listen to some of your favourites again. Can you say what styles they are in? What features of the song contribute to that style?

So where do you start?

When setting out to write a song, you may hit your first problem straight away. Should you start with the tune? The words? The chords? The rhythm? It can be difficult to decide which ingredient should come first in your writing process. Sometimes listening to your favourite songs can suggest a starting place. But it is often tricky to work out which element came first. Where do you begin?

Once you have written a few songs, you will see that you don't always start in the same place.

The answer is that different songwriters begin in different places. And each song has a different start in life. Paul McCartney says that he thought up the tune for *Yesterday* before the lyrics – so at the outset he simply sang "scrambled eggs" until the words fell into place. But with other songs he would have lyrics which were waiting for a tune. The secret is that it really doesn't matter where you begin – as long as you start somewhere. And the more you practise writing, the easier it becomes to generate ideas.

At the outset, begin where you feel most comfortable. It could be that you are good at thinking up tunes, but not words. In that case, go to the "Tunes" section and start there. If, on the other hand, you are happier writing words, go to the "Words" section first. Or you may want to find out about chords or rhythm first. Each section contains ideas about using your starting point to generate the other elements, so bit by bit you will want to move on to one of the other sections.

The "Chords" or "Rhythm" sections may be particularly helpful if you have played an instrument for a while but are just starting to write songs. Often just sitting down with your guitar or keyboard and playing can be a way of beginning a song. You will find that as you play your instrument more (this includes your voice if you're a singer), you will become more versatile, and able to play and write things that you hadn't previously been able to. This will allow you to express yourself better, possibly in ways that nobody else has done before.

If you've never done any songwriting before, and just want some ideas to get you started, use the hints below.

Other hints about where to begin
On page 5 you noted down your reactions to the songs on the CD. If you still need hints deciding where to begin, your list might help.

Boyfriend (track 1) and *Get your groove on* (track 8) began life as rhythms. If you like either of these tunes best, or identified the rhythm as an important feature, begin with the section on Rhythm on page 28.

28

I can't live without you (track 2) and *You tore out my heart* (track 6) have melody as their most prominent feature. If either of these appealed to you most, go to the section on Tunes that starts on page 16.

16

Something to believe in (track 3) and *Too much fun* (track 7) started life as lyrics. Go to the Words section on page 10 if either of these are your favourite.

10

You take me away (track 4) and *Baby my heart* (track 5) started as chord sequences. If you noticed the chords and liked either of these songs, you may find that the section on Chords on page 22 is a good place to begin.

22

No preferences?
Then just read the book straight through. It will give you plenty of ideas. But keep listening to lots of music and thinking about why you like it or why you don't. This will help you develop your own skills as a writer.

Writing your ideas down

Before you begin writing songs, think about how are you going to remember your ideas. Recording them would be ideal, but that isn't always easy, particularly if you think of something and don't have recording equipment to hand. Obviously you can write down the words, but that may not be enough to help you remember how the song went when you come back to it the following day. You could write the tune down, but that needs some knowledge of music notation, which you may not have. If you are playing the guitar, writing chords down can be useful, but that can be hard if you don't know the names of the chords you have found. Rhythms can be very difficult to write down. So here are some practical hints to help you remember your ideas:

• Use pictures – you may not know how to write down the tune using music notation, but you should be able to draw! If you have a tune you wish to remember, just use simple lines to indicate where the melody rises and falls. You can indicate long notes by drawing longer lines, like this:

If you are writing on a computer using sequencing software, this kind of notation may already be familiar to you.

• Write down rhythms by thinking of the beat (the regular pulse) first and showing that in your diagram. Draw blobs on the page – an equal distance apart – to represent the beats. Tap the beat with one hand (or your foot) and your rhythm with the other. Then write down the rhythm in relation to the regular blobs, like this:

You could use a metronome or the drum machine on a keyboard to keep the regular pulse for you.

Chord writing can be done quite easily. If you are playing on guitar, you can simply use pictures again. If you look at some music, you will often see chord windows – pictures of guitar chords above the staves, looking something like this:

If you don't know the name of the chord you are playing, just draw it as you see it on the guitar. To show a chord higher up the neck, simply choose a fret as your starting point, and write that number at the top of the chord box. If there is an open string that you don't want to sound in your chord, mark it with an X at the top of the diagram.

X

fret 5

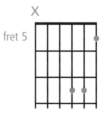

Once you have written down a chord in this way, you could look at the chord windows in any guitar book to see if it has a name.

If you are playing chords on a keyboard, you make a different sort of chord diagram. You don't need to draw the whole keyboard, as the pattern of black and white notes below is repeated all across the keyboard. You can then show the notes of your chord as dots:

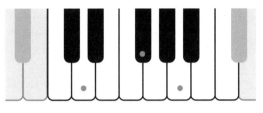

You could use this system to show a tune too. Instead of dots, use numbers to show the order in which the notes of your tune are played.

This kind of notation helps you to remember your ideas. It will also make it easier if you decide to record your song, because it really helps to have a clear idea of the exact melody, the chords and the rhythms. Writing down your song will also make you think about all of these things and can often improve your work.

Is this enough?

Notation systems like this can have their drawbacks. They are time-consuming to write or draw, and they take up a lot of space. Also, it may be hard for other people to read what you have written down. So while they work as shorthand to start with, if you decide to go further you may want to learn standard music notation. This allows you to notate your songs in the most complete way, so you can see everything that is happening at the same time and understand how all the parts of the song fit together. Look at the example below.

Read Music from Scratch, another book in this series, will help you learn to read and write music notation, whether or not you play a musical instrument.

This music shows the main parts of the song – words, tune, chords, rhythm – in a small space. For example, the chord in the keyboard diagram at the top of the page is expressed on the music notation by just one letter – D. The music is also shown in a form that anyone who reads music can understand. So, if you wanted to play your song with a backing band, you could give this notation to the musicians and they should be able to play it instantly.

Many songwriters manage very well without notation, preferring chord symbols and a good memory. But others find that as their writing skill grows, they need to use notation that everyone can understand. Some writers also say that music notation actually makes them more creative because they don't have to worry about remembering their work – they can notate it exactly.

Words: rhyme and rhythm

A song without lyrics isn't a song – it's just a piece of music. Most popular music has at least some lyrics. Think about the current charts: nearly all the songs have lyrics. The exercises below will prepare you for the lyric-writing activities over the page.

First, decide what you want to write about. Most lyrics are about specific subjects. Many pop songs are about love, getting together, breaking up and so on. Topics like this are popular because most people have feelings about them. But there are plenty of other subjects too. For example, many pop and rock songs protest against political injustices like war and poverty. Blues songs are often about personal misfortune. Dance music often contains a simple, positive message. But most lyrics stem from what the writer knows about, and that is always the place to begin. Make a list of a few topics that you know about and want to write about.

Does your song have to rhyme?

Think about some songs you like; most of them will rhyme. Rhyme is important because it gives the words a "shape" which helps when you come to think about the music. If you look at the words of a song, you will see which lines rhyme with each other. Below are three very common rhyme schemes: ABAB (alternate lines rhyme); ABCB (second and fourth lines rhyme) or rhyming couplets (lines next to each other rhyme).

Here's ABAB:

> *If you were mine,*
> *You'd be my lady forever.*
> *Sweeter than wine,*
> *I would love you more than treasure.*

*"Forever" and "treasure" is a **half-rhyme** – the words don't rhyme exactly but they sound similar. Most half-rhymes work well when they are sung.*

An ABCB sequence looks like this:

> *Hope is never lost*
> *And life ain't really blue*
> *The time has come to live*
> *Let courage see you through*

And a rhyming couplet sequence looks like this:

> *Lately, I'm finding it hard to go to sleep;*
> *I'm tossing and turning and it's making me feel weak.*
> *I just can't take it, said it's driving me insane;*
> *I need you to need me, oh, I can't take much more pain.*

Choose a few songs you know and write out some lyrics from each one. Look for any rhymes. Can you find examples of ABAB, ABCB and rhyming couplets? You may find other patterns too, and songs that divide up into groups of more (or fewer) than four lines. Can you find any songs that don't rhyme at all?

Words and their rhythm

As well as rhyme, you need to think about the rhythms your words create. All words, whether spoken or sung, have a natural rhythm, but the spoken version may be different from what you sing. Take the words to "Jack and Jill". If you were just speaking them, you would stress some words, making them sound more important than the others. Below, the words in CAPITALS are the ones you would probably stress in natural speech.

JACK and JILL went up the HILL to fetch a pail of WATER.

But in the song the stresses are slightly different. The meaning is the same, but now the words fit with the rhythm of the tune:

JACK and JILL went UP the HILL,
To FETCH a PAIL of WA-ter

Jack and Jill's names, where they are going and their action are all stressed. This is not how you would speak it, but it still stresses the meaningful words and leaves the filler words unstressed. (For example, 'fetch' has meaning on its own, but 'to' and 'the' are filler words which need other words around them to have any meaning.)

Now say the words below, with the stresses as marked. Feel how odd it sounds:

Jack AND Jill WENT up THE hill,
TO fetch A pail OF waTER

The same is true if you stress the wrong words in your own lyrics. Their meaning might be lost because the listener will not hear what you're saying, only the strange way you've said it. The way to avoid this is to look at the words you've written and ask yourself how you would speak them. Listen out for the words you stress, as these are probably the ones to stress in your song.

Speak the lyrics below and mark the words that you stress. (Don't mark the words you think you should stress; just the words you actually stress!)

I've been watching you for so, so long,
Boyfriend, my boyfriend.
You got the looks and you got it goin' on,
Boyfriend, my boyfriend.

You probably found yourself stressing the important words. There are several ways to do this that will all sound fine.

Now try putting the stresses on the filler words instead. It sounds odd, because you are putting stresses on words that you wouldn't stress in normal conversation.

Words: writing lyrics

Now it's time to write some lyrics. To get you started, answer the questions below.

1) What do I want to write about? (Love, relationships, pigeons, anything – it doesn't matter, just make a start!)

2) What do I want to say about the subject? (It could be positive or negative, personal or general.)

3) What words are associated with that subject? (Make a list of the words that immediately spring to mind. Other words or even sentences may then become obvious. Write everything down!)

Don't worry if your list looks odd at first.

4) When you look at the list of words, do any rhymes come to mind immediately that will make sense in the song?

5) Do I want long lines or short lines? (This ties in with the rhythm of the words, and will often be influenced by the music, if you are using that as a starting point.)

6) Using these words and ideas, try writing one verse

Here's an example:

1) What do I want to write about? Relationships, love

2) What do I want to say about the subject? Sad, just broke up, personal

3) What words are associated with that subject? Down, since you've been away, lonely, empty, low, pain

4) When you look at the list of words, do any rhymes come to mind that will make sense in the song? You/through, pain/again, use 'gone' for 'away', then make gone/one a half-rhyme

5) Do I want long lines or short lines? A mixture

6) Using these words and ideas, try writing one verse.

> *It's cold and lonely once again.*
> *Don't know if I can stand the pain.*
> *I really needed you,*
> *Suppose that I still do*
> *The same.*

The last line just happened as a result of the first four. When this happens, keep the idea and work around it. These extra thoughts are part of your individuality as a writer.

Look at the rhymes. Lines 1 and 2 rhyme, as do lines 3 and 4 (rhyming couplets). The final short line is a half-rhyme ("same" with "pain"). If you say the words to yourself, and think carefully about the stress and the rhythms, the short final line suggests something really sad and emotional.

Another example – less emotional this time!

1) What do I want to write about? Pigeons

2) What do I want to say about the subject? Happiness, joy at seeing and feeding pigeons, relaxation

3) What words are associated with that subject? Food, bread, calm, coo, smile, wings, flap, sun

4) When you look at the list of words, do any rhymes come to mind immediately that will make sense in the song? Half-rhyme of 'coo' and 'food'; 'smile' could rhyme with 'while' (which comes to mind from 'calm' – as in spending a while relaxing).

Long vowel sounds like "ooh" and "aah" can make a song sound relaxed.

5) Do I want long lines or short lines? Long lines sound relaxed

6) Using these words and ideas, try writing one verse:

I think I'll go and spend a while,
With my grey friends who coo,
They always seem to make me smile
I feed them near the zoo.

Clearly any song about pigeons is going to be fairly light-hearted in tone. That immediately suggests a particular style of music. Imagine what sort of music you'd expect with these words.

Words into rhythm, rhythm into music
Speak your own words and mark the ones that you stress. Do they feel natural when you say them? Do they suggest a rhythm? If so, try writing the rhythm down (use the method on page 8 if you don't know music notation). Then say your words in rhythm a few times. Does the rise and fall of the notes begin to suggest a tune?

30

A few more hints
• Good words can sometimes sound odd or silly when you turn them into song lyrics. To avoid this, always read the words as if you were speaking them before you start thinking about a rhythm.
• Don't rearrange the order of the words to force lines to rhyme if the result sounds unnatural – this is worse than using lines that don't rhyme at all.

Lyrics or poetry?
Write down some of the lyrics to a current chart song and read them back without the music. They probably look and sound a bit strange. This is because lyrics are not the same as poetry. They are part and parcel of the song itself – they were created to fit with the melody, the chords and the rhythm. Lyrics follow some of the rules of poetry you may have learned at school, but they have other features besides. Bear this in mind when you start writing.

Some song lyrics do work without their music. Listen to (and read) some songs by Bob Dylan, Joni Mitchell and Smokey Robinson

Words: turning lyrics into songs

In a way it's simple. You just keep writing until you have said what you want to say. The second verse is often easier, because you may have ideas left over from the first. But now you need to think about the shape of your song (usually called its structure) – how the verses build up into the finished product.

As with rhyme schemes, most songs follow one of a few standard structures. The simplest of these is *verse-chorus*. The chorus is normally the most memorable part of the song, with the most instantly recognisable tune, the strongest rhymes and the most important lyrics. It is repeated several times during the song, usually after each new verse.

See page 18 for more about writing tunes for choruses.

VERSE
If you were mine,
You'd be my lady forever.
Sweeter than wine,
I would love you more than treasure.
You're so precious, I need you in my life.

Can you sing the chorus to Baby my Heart? If not, remind yourself of what it sounds like by listening to track 5

CHORUS
Baby, my heart it beats for you,
When you're not here it breaks in two.
I long for the day when you will stay,
Forever and ever and a day.

Here's a slightly more complex structure: verse, verse, chorus.

VERSE 1
It's cold and lonely once again.
Don't know if I can stand the pain.
I really needed you,
Suppose that I still do
The same.

When writing the music for this song, you would want the two verses to have the same melody.

VERSE 2
I'm standing by what I believe;
I cannot bring myself to leave.
It seems to burn inside,
This feeling I can't hide –
D'you see?

Can you see how the two verses have the same rhyme scheme? This helps to hold the song together.

CHORUS
Every time I breathe, I cannot believe
We're still standing after all the years.
All the hurt and pain I'd live through again,
By understanding why we both shed those tears.
But if it's time for us to drift apart,
There'll be just one thing that's on my mind.
I've been wondering
Why you tore out my heart.

*"Breathe / believe" and "pain / again" are called **internal rhymes** as they come within one line of the verse. They help to make the chorus more memorable.*

More complicated structures

A *pre-chorus* comes between the verse(s) and the chorus. Often this will be fairly short (two lines) and will lead in to the chorus, both melodically and lyrically. An example:

VERSE
Lately, I'm finding it hard to go to sleep;
I'm tossing and turning and it's making me feel weak.
I just can't take it, said it's driving me insane;
I need you to need me, oh, I just can't take the pain.

PRE-CHORUS
Oh, the joy, when I speak your name; feels so good inside.
Oh, the joy, when I see your face. I can't wait to make you mine.

CHORUS
You take me away into the clouds where I'm in love.
When I'm in your arms I feel a special kind of love.
I never knew that I could have someone like you.
But like in a dream I know things really can come true.

More about structures

There are no real rules about song structures, but very experimental structures can make your song hard to understand. Verse/chorus or verse/verse/chorus are satisfying structures that make a song feel complete, so you will probably return to them again and again.

Try expanding some of the ideas for lyrics that you wrote on page 12. Write more verses, decide on a chorus, and write everything down as a complete song with a beginning, a middle and an end.

Turning structures into songs

The structure of your lyrics will affect your melody, too. Obviously, if you have a pre-chorus section in the lyrics, you will need a pre-chorus melody to go with it. But deciding which of your words are verses and which are choruses will help you when you come to add the music, as the structure of the words and music will be the same.

A few more hints

• As you begin to write more, you may find that some words you had intended as a verse work better as a chorus, or the other way round. Don't hesitate to try these things.
• At first, try to give verse words and chorus words similar rhythms. Try to move as smoothly as possible from verse to chorus. When you read the lyrics to your complete song aloud, does it feel as though you have to change the natural rhythm of the words? If so, this will make the whole song feel disjointed.
• If you are still struggling with lyric writing, you may wish to start songwriting somewhere else. It is often the case that once you have a chord sequence or a melody, the words naturally appear, fitting in with the mood and rhythm of the music you have created.

Several songs on Jeff Buckley's album Grace *have complicated but successful song structures. So do* Paranoid Android *by Radiohead and Queen's* Bohemian Rhapsody.

A rhythm change in the middle of a song can sometimes add extra interest. Listen to Englishman in New York *by Sting, or the album* Swoon *by Prefab Sprout.*

Tunes

There is no single way to write a tune. Let's begin by looking at writing a melody on its own. This may seem quite daunting without chords or lyrics to start you off, but the outcome can be very successful. If you write a tune this way you will think about every single note, and the result will sound confident and well-organised. And if you are struggling with chords or lyrics as a starting point, starting with a melody may well suggest chords and lyrics as you are writing it.

Start by choosing your first note – either sing it or play it on an instrument. Choose one that is comfortable to sing or play (a starting note is very rarely the highest note of a tune, so leave some room!). Then sing a melody of just a few notes. Don't worry about which bit of the song you are writing. When you are happy with your notes, jot them down using the line method on page 8, or music notation if you know it.

An example (line method and music – listen to track 9):

Once you have your first group of notes like this (called a phrase), see if it suggests an answering group, either similar to the first phrase or in contrast to it. Try singing an answering phrase to track 9 before you look at and listen to the version below.

Once you have written two phrases and combined them, you are well on the way to your first complete melody. In a way, this is the hardest part – the rest is all about developing your original idea.

Wait half an hour, then try singing your phrases from memory. Writing a memorable melody is one of the most important parts of songwriting and, unless you are very gifted, one which you may have to work on. So keep practising and write some more.

Here are two more opening phrases. Can you sing or play your own continuations for each of them? First, make the continuations like the given phrases, using notes which are the same or similar. Then experiment with writing continuations that are different from the given phrases. Write your continuations down.

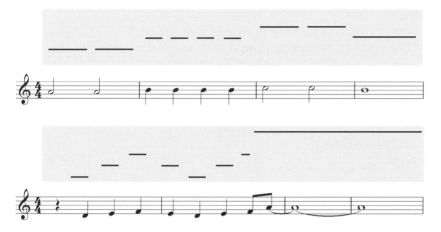

Now do this from scratch – make up your own opening phrases and write some continuations. Do this lots of times until you have plenty of material to choose from.

Once you have your first two phrases, your next job is to extend your melody. Popular music often contains some repetition. You may find that repeating (or slightly varying) the first phrase will give you the third, and that the fourth can be created from the second. Also, the idea of continuation phrases can be extended to groups of phrases – so that when you sing or play the first group of phrases, you may find yourself thinking of a second.

Take the phrases and continuations from the exercises above, and make up third and fourth phrases to go with them. Again, try similar phrases (this should be fairly easy), then try ones which are deliberately different (this could be harder). Try phrases with fewer notes held for longer, with more notes sung quicker, phrases which are higher, lower, and so on.

Melodies and lyrics
The way that phrases are repeated in melodies is similar to the way that words rhyme in lyrics. Just as some lines rhyme with each other and others don't, so some phrases are similar to each other and others are quite different. When adding a melody to lyrics it can help to match the phrase repetitions to the rhyme scheme. When adding lyrics to a melody, it is useful to bear in mind the phrase repetitions when thinking up your rhymes.

Listen to some of your favourite songs and think about the music. Are there repeated phrases? If so, can you write down the pattern of repeats?

Tunes: expanding your ideas

Now that you have written a few groups of four phrases, it is time to develop these into verses and choruses. In some ways this is easier, as you have the initial idea. Now you need to think about the shape of your song (usually called its structure) and about building the groups of phrases into the finished product.

What have you written?

Go back to the melodies that you wrote on the previous page. Play or sing them again and choose your favourite. Does it feel as if it is leading to some other music (a verse), or does it feel like the central part of a song that everyone will remember (the chorus)? If you think you've written a chorus, carry on to the section below. If you think you've written a verse, skip to the section opposite called "About verses". If you're not sure, don't worry – just keep going. Things will get clearer as you continue.

About choruses

The chorus is the part of the song that people go away singing. Does your group of phrases sound like this? Sometimes you will find that you have written a memorable chorus without really trying, but usually it will need a bit of help if it is really going to do the job. Here are a few tips about tweaking your melody to make a suitable chorus:

• A chorus often contains repetition of the tune (or part of it), the rhythm or the lyrics, or all three – this helps people remember it. So if a particular phrase appears to work, you might think about repeating it.

• A chorus is usually simple, and often quite short. If you like your melody but feel that it has too much variety, or that it is too long, you might want to remove part of it (don't throw it away – use it in the verse instead!).

• A chorus is often at a higher pitch than the verses. This adds an extra touch of vocal intensity and excitement. (If your phrases sound a bit dull, try singing them higher – this may well help.)

• A chorus often contrasts with the rest of the song in some way (bear this in mind when you come to write the verses).

You could have written a quiet, low, complicated, long tune which would work well as a chorus. But ask yourself whether you should really make that part the verse instead. Your chorus must be memorable. If you can remember the melody the next day without looking at your notes, you're most of the way there. It may take you a while to get used to writing choruses, but if you bear the points above in mind, you should be on your way to succeeding.

Once you have a chorus melody that you are happy with, you need to write a verse to go with it.

About verses

The verse is usually the part that people hear first, so it needs to draw listeners into the song. Verse melodies often feel as if they are leading somewhere. If you think your melody is like this, here are some tips for developing it into a verse:

• A verse often 'builds' towards the chorus. In the last phrase of your verse, try making the melody rise, or have more, faster notes.

• Experiment with repeating and varying phrases to build tension towards the chorus. For example, if your melody consists of two phrases each sung twice, try changing the order in which they are sung. "Phrase a, phrase b, phrase a, phrase b," will sound very different from "Phrase a, phrase b, phrase b, phrase a".

• You can make verses more complex than choruses. If you want to insert an extra line (which you may, when you come to add lyrics), it's usually better to do this in the verse than the chorus.

• A verse often contrasts with the rest of the song in some way (bear this in mind when you come to write the chorus).

Once you have a verse melody you are happy with, write a chorus to go with it. Go back to "About choruses" opposite.

Putting verses and choruses together

It is very likely that any one of the melodies you wrote on page 17 will contain enough ideas to develop into both a verse and a chorus. Experiment with repetition, with variation and with contrast until you have two separate but linked groups of phrases, one of which really appears to lead into the other. Here's an example of a verse and a chorus (listen to track 13 of the CD):

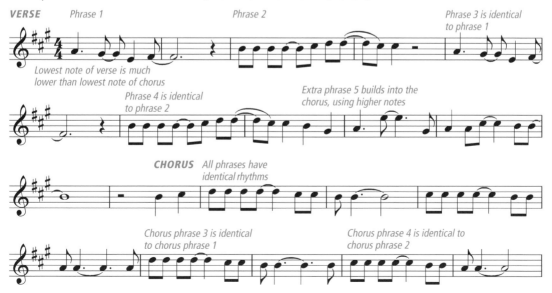

Tunes: turning melodies into songs

Now that you have a verse melody and a chorus melody, you can build them into an entire song. Just as you turned notes into opening phrases and answering phrases, then developed these into verses and choruses, you join verses and choruses together in different patterns to make songs. Most songs follow one of a few standard patterns or structures.

The most common structure is *verse-chorus*. In this pattern, the chorus is repeated several times, usually after each verse. In the simplest verse-chorus songs, the only thing that changes as the song progresses are the words in the verse. Everything else stays the same. Many folk songs use this structure. It works well if the words are very important (for instance if the song is telling a story). Try alternating your verse melody and your chorus melody a few times.

In more complicated verse-chorus songs, the melody for each verse is slightly different – the rhythm or the tune might change slightly (to fit with different words, for example). This often helps people remember the chorus better, as it is the part they identify each time it comes round. Try your melody again, this time making slight alterations to the verse each time but keeping the same chorus.

You might find as you sing or play your song back that you want some extra music too. You might feel as though you need some more variation to make the melody more interesting. In some songs you will find a linking section called a *bridge*. It often comes before you hear the chorus for the second time. Sometimes it has words, but sometimes it is an instrumental section with no singing. Sing or play your melody again. Do you want to write an extra section?

*Another extra section, the **coda**, comes right at the end and is the last thing you hear. Some songs need a section like this to make them feel complete.*

Here are some typical song structures. First, try playing your own melodies following these schemes.

Verse 1 • Verse 2 • Chorus • Verse 3 • Chorus • Chorus

Verse 1 • Chorus • Verse 2 • Chorus • Bridge • Chorus • Chorus

Chorus • Verse 1 • Chorus • Verse 2 • Chorus • Bridge • Chorus • Chorus

Also listen to the songs on the CD and see if you can identify any of the structures above. Then listen to some of your favourite songs and work out their structures. The more you do this, the more familiar you will become with how songs work. Make a note of anything you hear which is unusual – whether or not you like it!

Above all, keep experimenting with melodies and structures. If you want to write a song that never repeats any section, then try it! To generate more ideas for tunes, return to page 16 and work through the exercises once more. When you have done this a few times you will feel more confident about writing melodies of your own that you feel happy with.

For an example of a successful song that doesn't really have any verse or chorus structure at all, listen to Praying for Time *by George Michael.*

Hints and tips

It can be difficult to keep thinking up ideas for new melodies, and sometimes it can be tricky to think up variations of existing ones. Here are a few hints, tips and exercises to help you. Try them all at least once – they will stimulate your ability to create melodies. And remember, your first idea isn't always your best!

• If you have an idea for a melody but don't think it is working, try changing one note here or there. Minor alterations can make all the difference. Move a note up or down, miss a note out, add in an extra one and so on. Change the rhythm.

• If a melody sounds uninteresting fast, try slowing it down. Or speed up a slow tune. Try it higher or lower, in a different part of your voice or starting on a different note of your instrument.

• If you don't know where to go with a phrase, try singing it backwards. Sometimes the backwards version is a good answer to the forwards one. Sometimes you may prefer the backwards version and want to get rid of the forwards one! Or try using the forwards version for the verse, and the backwards one for the chorus.

• Write everything down, even ideas that feel unimportant at the time. Don't waste anything – phrases often resurface in a different form even months later.

• Sing your melodies to other people. Get them to sing them back to you (this is a good test of how memorable your phrases are). Sometimes people change tunes when they sing them back, and this might be just the key to the melody you are looking for.

Words with melodies

By this stage, the development of your song will also begin to depend on the words. This is the point at which the two elements begin to work together. If you have begun by writing a melody, it is important now – even if you don't actually write any words yet – to understand the structure of your melody so that you know how to fit words to it when the time comes.

Write down the plan of your melody, listing the verses, the choruses, any bridge material and any sections that you have imagined as instrumentals. Within each section, make a note of any phrases that repeat and any that are variations of each other. If you have an extra phrase in your verse melody, make a note of the fact.

In practice you will find a number of things happen. Firstly, as you are writing your melody, words may suggest themselves too – even before you begin the activities on pages 10–15. If they do, write them down. Secondly, if you begin writing words to a finished melody you may well find that you will want to alter it, not the words, to make it all fit together.

Chords

A chord is any group of two or more notes played at the same time. Even when you only have a single bass note played underneath a single melody note, you have a chord. Chords (sometimes also called harmony) are the building blocks of a song, even though they can be the part that attracts the least attention. (Even unaccompanied songs like folk ballads are usually based around chords that the melody suggests to the listener.) And chords can be the starting point for a song, as much as the tune or the words.

The information in these pages assumes you know something about playing chords. If you are playing the guitar or electronic keyboard, you probably do this already and will be familiar with notation like chord windows and chord symbols. Otherwise, the music notation on these pages is enough to get you started.

You can find out about chords in the other books in this series, Keyboards from Scratch, Guitar from Scratch *and* Read Music from Scratch.

Start with a few individual chords first, using the notation below. Try them slowly on a guitar or a keyboard, using the symbols, or play them from the music. Play each one a few times before you move on to the next. (You can hear these chords on track 14 of the CD, too.) It's important just to hear how the notes in each chord fit together. Once you have concentrated on these you will know what you are listening for in other songs.

*In this book, the symbol **C** means a chord of C major, while **Cm** means C minor.*

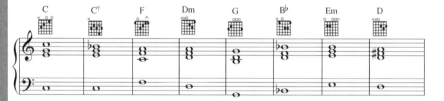

*A chord is usually named after its lowest note, called its **root**.*

Grouping chords together

Chords fit together in groups to make a framework for a song. These groups are called chord progressions. There are many standard chord progressions that are used over and over again in pop songs, just as there are standard rhyme schemes for words and standard ways of repeating patterns of phrases to form melodies. As with words and tunes, it can help to begin with some of the standard schemes before you move on to writing your own. Here's one of the most common chord progressions of all:

C   C   C   C7   F   F   C   C   G   F   C   C

You can find the notes and chord windows for all these chords in the music above.

This progression is known as 12-bar blues. Blues has origins in ancient African and American folk music, and blues progressions are the backbone of an enormous number of songs. 12-bar is simple but also extremely flexible – it can be used in many different ways. Play it a few times. Keep a steady beat and play each chord four times. Then vary it by playing it faster or slower, then by playing three beats in a bar instead of four, or to a more complex rhythm. Try it in different keys too – use chords of **A**, **A7**, **D** and **E**, for example. You will see that the "feel" changes a lot as you alter these things.

Bill Haley's Rock around the clock *uses this chord progression, as do many blues and rock-and-roll songs. Listen to Muddy Waters or Fats Domino for some examples.*

There's something very "logical" about 12-bar blues – every chord seems to be followed by exactly the right one. This may be because 12-bar is so common that it feels "natural".

If we look at 12-bar blues in detail, we will see more about how chord progressions work. Can you divide it up into smaller units? Do some of the chords fall into groups with others? 12-bar divides very conveniently into three groups of four. Play the progression once more, this time leaving a gap after every four bars. Think about each four-bar section.

- Section one consists of four repeated **C** chords, with a 7th added in the last. This repetition builds tension before the second section (repetition to build tension is a common and very effective songwriting device).

- Section two (**F**, **F**, **C**, **C**) changes the chord, but then returns us to the **C** chord.

- Section three (**G**, **F**, **C**, **C**) gives us a high point of tension (**G**) and then a return, via **F**, to the **C** chord (called a resolution).

It may seem strange to talk of "tension" and "resolution", but these terms are useful when talking about chords. Most progressions are based on a "home" chord where the song feels "centred" or "at home". Whenever the progression moves to a different chord, it moves away from the home chord and this creates tension until it returns. Any progression creates these tensions and resolutions.

Famous examples of tension/resolution: the opening bars of David Bowie's Space Oddity *or* Wonderwall *by Oasis. Listen to* Play Dead *by Björk, too.*

Create your own progressions. Use the chords **C**, **F** and **G**. Choose two of the chords and use them to play a pattern three times. Then play a final pattern that includes the third chord. For example:

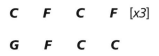

C   **F**   **C**   **F**   [*x3*]

G   **F**   **C**   **C**

Which is the home chord in this progression?

More about "home" chords

In most progressions, only one chord will feel like the home chord. This is usually the chord that finishes the song, and often the first chord too. In music theory, this chord is called the *tonic*, or sometimes the *key chord*. The tonic in the blues progression opposite is **C**, because that chord feels like the home chord.

Most pop songs emphasise the tonic chord so that they have a strong sense of being "rooted". When playing chord progressions or making up your own, it helps to get a feel for which is the tonic. Listen to some of your favourite songs. Try to point out when the tonic chord is being played and when you are hearing another chord instead. How often do you hear the tonic chord in relation to the others? Can you play these chords on the guitar or keyboard, and can you name them?

In some songs, it can be hard to identify the tonic. This creates an unsettling, mysterious effect. Listen to Amelia *by Joni Mitchell for an example of this, or Radiohead's* Pyramid Song.

Grouping chords into chord progressions

The 12-bar blues on page 22 is an example of a common chord progression that works well over a large number of bars. While many songs are based on entirely new and individual progressions, the most successful ones have clear progressions that are easy for the listener to understand. On these pages you can find out some more about how to group chords into progressions.

Starting from scratch

If you are building a progression from scratch as the first step in writing a song, don't use too many chords. Start with just two or three. Put small groups of chords together in short sections, then join these up to make larger patterns. Begin with two chords that sound good together, then add others as you need them to create the tension/resolution effects described on the previous page.

Need some suggestions to get you started? Try:

C   Am   G
or
G   C   D
or
G   Em   C   D

Play the chords on page 22 in any order and see if you like any of the combinations. Once you have a group of chords that you like for your first line, decide how to continue it. The easiest option is to repeat it. This technique is used in countless pop songs. Another option is to find contrasting chords to follow it. For example:

Em   D   Em   D

G   C   G   G

Can you hear how the second line seems to "answer" the first?

This pattern works well because you don't hear the tonic (**G**) until line 2 – tension in the first, resolution in the second. There are theories about chords and which work well together, and you can read these in any music theory book. But in reality the best way of inventing a chord progression is to sit down and play chords. Listen carefully until you find ones that go together. Make sure you write your progressions down, either with symbols or in music notation.

Very often, you will "feel" when a progression is right. You may spend a while searching for the chord you want – you might not even know its name – but you will know when you find it. (This is a common experience even among professional songwriters.) It might seem odd at first to search for chords like this, but it's how you build progressions that sound right to you. And remember, if they sound right to you, they probably sound right to other people too.

Building up

Now you have your first two lines, choose what to do next. Again, the simplest thing is to repeat them – this is common in pop songs. But for the repeat you could reverse the order of the chords within the lines, swap the lines around, or swap half of line two with half of line one. Experiment a bit. It's likely that, once again, you will "know" when you have the right continuation.

Don't forget to write everything down. Progressions you reject today could well be perfect for your next song!

At first, you will probably feel most comfortable with four-bar lines. This is because so many songs follow this pattern. A 12-bar blues is based on three four-bar lines. Other songs use 8- or 16-bar progressions (two four-bar lines or four four-bar lines).

Line by line

Make some more chord progressions of your own, either with the chords on page 22 or any others that you know.

- Find two or three chords that sound good together

- Create your first line of four bars

- Find an "answering" line using the same chords or different ones

- When you have a group of two lines, work out whether to repeat them to make lines three and four, or whether you need two different lines to complete your progression

Try to use both major and minor chords.

Play your progressions many times, changing a chord here and there, experimenting with different combinations.

Where do you stop?

Some dance music is based on just one chord, with maybe a second one every so often for contrast. This sounds right because there are other things going on – rhythm, interesting textures and so on. Many songs sound fine with just two chords – it depends on the style of music. Others use longer progressions, but repeat them over and over again (this is how 12-bar blues works). Many songs have one progression for the verse, one for the chorus. Some have one or two others as well – for the bridge and the coda.

Roadrunner by Jonathan Richman uses two chords for eight minutes – but listen to what happens at the end! Listen to Me in Honey by REM as well – it has just one chord for the verse, one for the chorus.

20

When you are writing a progression, you will know when it feels complete. You will also know whether a particular progression needs to be followed by another one. Some progressions feel self-contained, others lead on to something else. Look at this one:

Cm	*Cm*	*Cm*	*Cm*
Cm	*Cm*	*Cm*	*Cm*
Fm	*Cm*	*Fm*	*Cm*
Fm	*Cm*	*D*	*G*

Do you recognise this progression? It is the opening of Boyfriend, on track 1 of the CD. Do you remember what happens next?

21

The repetition of the first chord for eight bars creates a lot of tension. There is a sort of resolution in the third line, but the repeated **Fm Cm** seems to push on to the last line. The **D G** doesn't return to the home chord. The progression feels finished but seems to want to move somewhere else. What happens next? It doesn't work just to go back to the beginning and play the sequence again. It doesn't work just to play the tonic chord. What it needs is a second progression to balance the first one. Can you invent one?

The best way to get a feel for chord progressions is to listen to lots of songs, particularly ones you really like. Ideally write the chords down of a favourite song and play around with them. Add your own chords in certain places to see what the difference is. This may well give you ideas for your own songs.

You may find it difficult to work out the chords just from listening, but why not try and see which chords you know that will fit under the melody?

Turning chord progressions into songs

Some songs use only one progression, but many use more than one. The song below is in three sections, each with its own progression. Play these chords a few times, or listen to them on track 22. Can you spot the tonic chord? Can you hear the way each progression seems to lead to the next one?

22

Dm	Em	F	G
Dm	Em	F	G
Dm	Em	F	G
Dm	Em	F	G

Progression 1 (verse) builds tension by repeating the same chord pattern four times.

F	G	Am	Am
F	G	Am	Am
F	G	Am	Am
Dm		Esus	E

Progression 2 (pre-chorus) continues to build to the final line, where it is obviously leading to a new section.

F	G	C	C
F	G	C	C
F	G	C	C
F	G	C	C

Progression 3 (chorus) feels like a "resolution" where the tonic chord (C) is finally reached.

Making choices

When you have some progressions you like, play them a few times. What happens if you change a chord here and there? Or add an extra bar to increase tension? Does it still sound right if you change the order of your progressions? If a progression is repeated, what happens if you vary the number of repetitions? Experiment to find versions of progressions and songs that you like best.

You can do this with the chords above. Try altering the order of the sections. There are six possibilities – which sounds best? And what happens if you alter one or two chords?

Other changes may make big differences too. Playing your chords faster or slower can alter the character of the music completely. If you use minor chords instead of major, or major instead of minor, you will create a completely new effect. Altering the rhythm or the beat – playing three beats in a bar instead of four, for example – can start you off on a completely new train of thought.

What happens to the sequence above if you substitute C for every Dm? Or D for every Dm?

62

Beyond chords

You could write chords for a whole song (like the ones above, for example) before thinking about the words and tune. But even if you start out this way, chords quickly generate ideas for the other elements. If you have got this far with chords, you may have ideas for lyrics and melody. If so, looking at these sections now might help you to develop these.

10
16

It is likely that your words and tune will influence your final choice of chords. For example, your words may fall into a verse/chorus format. So, if you have two chord progressions, try using one for the verse and one for the chorus. If you have decided that you want a bridge section, you may need another progression for that, too. These are decisions that you can't make until you begin to put the different elements together.

14
20

Chords into melodies

Choose any chord progression – one you have written, or one on any of the previous pages. Play it a few times, either on the CD or your instrument. Once you are familiar with the chords, try singing a tune over the top. You will see that it is quite easy to find a tune to go with them, as some notes will work better with the chords than others. In a way, the chords "dictate" the melody – or maybe even several melodies. The melody may also suggest lyrics. The more you practise this, the easier it becomes.

Always write your melodies down so that you don't forget them.

Adding chords to an existing tune

What happens if you have invented a tune (using the activity on page 17, for example) but haven't added chords yet? First, find the tonic chord of your tune – this is usually the last note. If your tune ends on C, your tonic chord will probably be C as well. This is the chord to return to in order to make the song sound complete. Now sing your melody a few times and experiment with other chords beneath it. Some will work, some won't. This may feel a bit "hit and miss" at first, but all songwriters do it. Again, practice helps.

Some groups of chords work particularly well together. If your tonic is a major chord, try the major chords based on the fourth and fifth notes up from the tonic, and the minor chords based on the second, third and sixth notes. But you don't have to restrict yourself to these – some of the most interesting songs are based on unconventional chord progressions.

*If your tonic is **C**, try using the major chords of **F** and **G** and the minor chords of **Em** and **Am** to go with your melody. If your tonic is **D**, try using **G** and **A** major, and **F♯** and **B** minor.*

How many chords do you need to know?

The more chords you know, the wider your range of expression. You will be able to write more interesting progressions and, as a result, more interesting melodies too. You should always be on the lookout for new chords and new types of chord: major, minor, sevenths, chords with different bass notes and so on. A list of chords – like you find in a guitar or keyboard book – will help you. Some books also list groups of related chords based around a particular tonic – it can be useful to familiarise yourself with these.

If you change some of the chords you can gradually create a new chord progression that might suggest new melodies.

You should also think about voicings – how the notes of a chord are played together. Sometimes, when writing a progression, you may feel that a particular note ought to be at the top or bottom of a chord. You may already have found yourself missing out certain notes on the keyboard or strings on the guitar to make it sound more "right". Certain voicings are more popular in certain styles of music than others. Use chord charts, your instrument, and your ear to familiarise yourself with different voicings.

*These diagrams show two different voicings of the same **C** chord.*

Even without knowing about music theory, you will find that some chords are easy to play and sound good. A chord chart will show you other versions of the chord that you might not have thought of or played; try them. Sometimes learning a new chord – or even a new version of a chord – can inspire an entirely new song.

Rhythm

What comes to mind when you think about rhythm as part of a song? The drums? The drums and bass? The strumming on a guitar? The rhythm of the piano part? The rhythm of the melody? Actually, you should be thinking about all of them – rhythm is vital to any song, and it is impossible to write one without it. So which elements of rhythm should you concentrate on when songwriting?

In many pop songs, the part you notice first is the beat – the steady pulse that keeps going throughout. This is what you tap your foot to and dance to. The bass drum often plays this beat – it is the basic component of a song's rhythm. This continuous beat is divided into groups called bars. Bars with four beats are the most common. This means that every fourth beat feels "stronger" than the others.

Listen to some of your favourite songs and tap the beat along with the music.

You can hear this sort of beat on track 23. After a while, over the top of the beat you will hear a more complicated pattern of longer and shorter sounds. This pattern is called a rhythm. It is written out below, both as blocks and as music notation. In the blocks, the beat is shown as the orange dots, while the longer and shorter sounds are shown as black squares.

In music notation, the beat is described by the numbers at the beginning, which are called the time signature. You will see a time signature at the beginning of the sheet music to most songs. There are two numbers in a time signature. The top one tells you how many beats there are in a bar, while the lower one tells you what type of beats they are.

The black squares are the rhythm – the pattern of longer and shorter sounds. The orange dots are the beat – the steady pulse that keeps going.

The top number means each bar contains four beats. The bottom number tells you the type of beat.

4
4

Why time signatures are important

When writing a song, you will often decide on a time signature without thinking about it. However, thinking about it specifically may help you shape the song before you even have any music at all. Different time signatures have different moods and characters.

Most pop songs are in 4/4 – in fact, every single dance track you can think of will be in this time signature. Listen to track 23 again, tapping the first beat of each bar with your foot and the others with your hand. You should feel that the beat you tap with your foot is "stronger" than the three "weaker" beats you tap with your hand.

Listen to any dance track and tap along; the rhythm will follow this 4/4 pattern. Try to identify the strong beat and the weaker beats.

However, you may want to try a different time signature. One of the most common is 3/4 – one strong beat in every three. Tap it yourself, accenting the first beat of the bar (use the foot and hand method – it works!). Try the beat first, then the rhythm, then listen to track 24.

Can you think of any songs that use a 3/4 time signature?

24

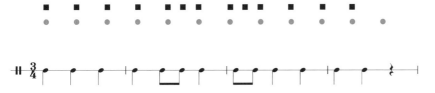

3/4 is the time signature used for waltzes. It is also common in folk music. A song with the rhythm above, when combined with folk instrumentation (acoustic guitars, tin whistles, accordions and so on) will sound convincingly 'folky'.

Another common time signature in popular music is 6/8; six short beats to a bar, usually grouped into two groups of three. Again, tap the beat, then the rhythm, then listen to track 25.

25

6/8 is similar to 3/4, but is quicker and more lively. It is often used in "rock ballads", the quieter songs that bands often put between the louder 4/4 songs. Because 6/8 is quite energetic, it doesn't sound like a waltz (which for a rock band is quite important!).

Make up your own rhythms using different time signatures. Keep the beat with your foot, and tap out patterns with your hands until you find some that you like. Write them down!

Tempo and accents
Your choice of time signature will most often be governed by your words (there is more about this over the page). But you will want to make choices about other aspects of your song's rhythm, too. One of the most important of these is the tempo – how fast or slow the beat is. The faster the beat, the faster the song will be. Faster tempos often sound lively and energetic – experiment with singing your own songs faster and slower.

Can you think of two versions of the same song, one faster and one slower? Which one do you prefer?

Think also about accents – where and how you emphasise different beats of the bar. Don't limit yourself to emphasising just the first beat of each bar – putting accents elsewhere in the bar will add energy to your song. Using the rhythms you made above, try altering the place where you put the accents. Each time you do this, you are making a new rhythm.

When you write out rhythms, you can use an accent symbol > to mark where you want the emphasised beats to be.

Rhythm and words

When you write rhythms, they may suggest their own words and tunes. But often you will have written words down before you even think much about their rhythm. We have already looked at how to make words sound natural by stressing the syllables that feel important. There is more about this below.

From lyrics to rhythm

When you have written some lyrics, you can use them to generate a rhythm. Here are the words to the chorus of *Get your groove on*. Keep a beat with your foot and say the words aloud to the beat.

> **You can get your groove on in the house tonight**
> **When you get your groove on you will feel alright**
> **We can dance and party 'til the morning light**
> **Get your groove on – groove on**

If the words won't fit to the beat, you may need to change the beat. Try it faster, slower, or even in a different time signature.

Mark the words where you want to place the biggest stress – underline them or put a ring round them. You may have to try this a few times before you get a pattern that works well for all four lines. This was my solution (though there are many others too):

> **<u>You</u> can get your <u>groove</u> on in the <u>house</u> to<u>night</u>**
> **<u>When</u> you get your <u>groove</u> on you will <u>feel</u> al<u>right</u>**
> **<u>We</u> can dance and <u>party</u> 'til the <u>morning</u> <u>light</u>**
> **Get your <u>groove</u> on – groove <u>on</u>**

As a general rule, the underlined words or syllables will fall on the strong beats of the bar – in 4/4, these are the first and third beats. The other words will fit round these. Here's the rhythm written out:

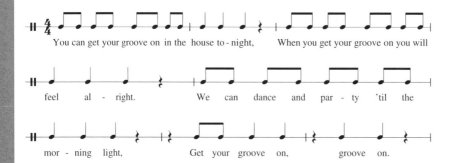

You can get your groove on in the house to-night, When you get your groove on you will feel al - right. We can dance and par-ty 'til the mor-ning light, Get your groove on, groove on.

Now try setting your own words to rhythm. Set up a steady beat and gradually add your words over the top, using the method above. It is likely that while writing the words you already had some rhythmic ideas, so begin with those. A good test is how easy it is to memorise your rhythm. If it is hard, try the following tricks:

Remember – stressed words should go on strong beats, less important ones on the weaker ones.

- rework the words slightly (add or remove a few)
- change the beat or rhythm you are working with
- stress different words
- change the length of the gaps between each line or phrase

Songs with unusual time signatures include Golden Brown *by the Stranglers, and Sting's* Seven Days.

Arranging your song

If you have got this far in the book, you may already have written at least one basic song, or parts of one. So far we have looked at the components of a song – the words, melody, chords and rhythm – and from page 34 onwards you will find a lot of information and activities about putting these together. But before that you need to think about a final element of songwriting: arranging.

When you write a song, you will probably play it many times. You may be happy with the sound of you and your guitar or keyboard, but this may not be what you have in mind for the final sound. Arranging (deciding what instruments to use for your song) is probably the last stage of songwriting. It may be less important to you if you just intend to play your song on your own. But you need to think about it if you are going to perform it with a band, or if you want to record it for anyone else to listen to – either your friends or a publisher or record company. Here are a few ideas:

59

Make a demo
It is always useful to make a rough recording (often known as a demo) of your song, if only to help you remember the words and music. The results will be very useful. For the first time, you will be able to stand back from performing the song and devote all your attention to listening to it.

There is a rough demo of Too much fun on track 26. Can you describe the differences between it and the full version on track 7?

26

07

Ask yourself the same questions about it that you did on page 5 about the songs on the CD. Answer honestly! What does the song sound like? Do you like it? Is it too fast? Too slow? Do the lyrics make sense? (Singing the words to a song and listening to them are entirely different. You know what the words are, but the listener doesn't.) Now is the best time to make any changes to things you don't like, and re-record if necessary. This is just for reference, but it will come in very handy later.

Thinking about arrangements
If you gave your finished song in its simplest form to someone else to perform, you might find that they changed it. It could end up in a different style, or at a different speed, or higher or lower, or with different chords that you hadn't thought of. There might be a big introduction added to it, or instrumental solos. All this comes into the realm of arranging.

Here are some examples of how an arrangement can completely change a song:

Steamy Windows, sung by Tina Turner as a rock epic, was originally sung by Tony Joe White, a country blues singer, on acoustic guitar

When you say nothing at all, sung by Ronan Keating in a pop style with fiddles and tin whistle, was also recorded by folk singer Alison Krauss. But it was originally a country tune by the singer Keith Whitley.

Your song as you have recorded it does have a basic arrangement already. You could leave it there: record a really good performance and say "that's it"! But you could go further, arranging it for any combination of musicians from a basic rhythm section (guitar, bass and drums, or keyboard, bass and drums) to a full orchestra. Whatever combination you choose, there is only one real rule – don't swamp the melody with too many instruments. Think about what your song really needs apart from your voice and an accompaniment instrument, and avoid the temptation to add in too many extras unless you really need them.

My Way was recorded by Frank Sinatra as a ballad and also by the Sex Pistols as a punk anthem.

Instrumentation

If you have a sound in your head that seems to work for your song, you've already started arranging. The trick is to get it on to the instrument that is best suited to the job. Acoustic instruments (instruments that don't need to be plugged in) are a good starting point. You can add virtually any single instrument – flute, oboe, clarinet, violin, viola, cello, trumpet, trombone, horn, and so on. A cello can be particularly useful because you get an expressive melody instrument that can also play flowing bass lines.

The oboe is unusual in pop music, but Rod Stewart's recording of Handbags and Gladrags shows how effective it can be.

You can sing or play lines to solo instrumentalists and they can try to play them for you. Notation would help, but it is possible to try out simple ideas by ear. Record or write down the results to use for reference later. Using acoustic instruments emphasises the fact that you don't need a full band to get expressive effects. Two or three instruments could add all the colour, rhythm and excitement that your song needs. Once you start bouncing ideas around with other players the magic really starts (future collaborators can be spotted at this point!).

One of the most expressive songs ever written, Yesterday by the Beatles, is very simply arranged for guitar and strings.

Playing your songs with a band

This can be hard to organise unless you can try your arrangement out with an existing band at one of their rehearsals. It would take all day to sing the parts you want to a six-piece band, so you will need to write something down in advance for the players – at least the melody and the chords. As long as everyone understands the notation you are using, it doesn't matter what you use. Experienced musicians can work from chords only, from standard music notation or by ear if really necessary (and if you have plenty of time!).

MIDI to the rescue

MIDI stands for Musical Instrument Digital Interface. It is a standard operating and communication system for electronic music devices, including keyboards, guitars, sound systems and mixing desks. MIDI has become the best tool for arranging since the invention of the piano. You can buy a MIDI keyboard for as little as £100.

You could use MIDI to control a full-blown Hollywood production, with dry ice, lasers and revolving stage!

The great thing about MIDI is that the brass section you've dreamed of adding to your song is sitting there in your keyboard. With just one MIDI keyboard, you will be able to choose from a list of at least 128 instruments and have up to 16 of them (including drums) playing at once. A part of the keyboard called the sequencer lets you record your instrumental parts one by one, play them back, change them if necessary, alter the volume levels and so on.

All the songs on the CD were recorded and arranged using MIDI.

If you have a computer and a music package which enables you to record and play back via MIDI and a keyboard, you may be able to record up to 72 tracks. Additionally you will be able to add in "real audio" – the actual sounds of voices, electric guitar, and acoustic instruments. You can store all your arrangements and recordings on your computer.

Recording an arrangement

If you don't have MIDI, you can use any recording equipment to experiment with arranging. You can sing and play along with your demo, working out other parts like extra vocals or instrumental lines. Write these parts down so that you don't forget them.

If you have more than one machine – such as a portable tape player and the tape deck on a stereo – you can add these extra parts to your demo. Play the demo back (preferably on whichever of your machines makes the best sound), and practise your extra parts by playing them over the top. Then, on the second machine, record the sound of the demo with you (or your instrumentalists) playing or singing along. Play it back to check it's what you had in mind.

You can continue adding to your recording by playing back the result (again, preferably on the machine that makes the best sound), adding more parts over the top and recording them on to your second machine. You can only do this two or three times – after this the sound quality will not be good enough – but that will be enough to hear the effects of adding in extra vocal parts or instruments. Using fresh tapes each time will improve your chances of success. It also means that you aren't recording over your earlier attempts, so you can always backtrack if something doesn't work.

Arrangements into songs

If you have an idea for a tune or chord progression, playing it on an instrument or a group of instruments can help the song to take shape. For example, instead of playing chords on piano, try them on guitar. Try starting your arrangement with the chorus melody played on a solo instrument. Different textures create variety and can be used to create tension, resolution and contrast, underlining the song's progression from one section to the next. Changing an instrument can change the mood of a song completely. If you experiment enough with textures and instruments you will find that these, too, begin to suggest chord progressions, rhythms and melodies of their own – even lyrics. So sometimes choosing instruments can be the starting point of an entire song.

If you are developing a complicated arrangement, it can help to write a chart showing exactly which instrument plays at what point in the song.

Some styles of arranging are instantly recognizable. The Motown recordings of the 1960s, or the Nashville sound of Billy Sherill in the 1970s are good examples.

Other things to think about

Apart from choosing the instruments that might play your song, other arranging matters include:

- Dynamics (which parts of the song should be loud, which soft?)
- Backing vocals (more than one other part singing behind the melody, with or without words)
- Counter melodies (tunes played at the same time as the main melody)
- Instrumental sections (introductions, solos, links, bridges)
- Stops (for example, stopping all the instruments during the last line of a chorus is a spectacular effect)
- Fills (to get gracefully from one section to the next)

The beginning of Roxy Music's Virginia Plain has a spectacular dynamic effect – so does the end of David Bowie's Space Oddity.

In Baker Street by Gerry Rafferty, or Song 2 by Blur, the instrumental section is almost as important as the vocals.

Songwriting in practice

By now you should be feeling more confident about creating ideas for each individual part of a song, and about using one element of a song to generate ideas for another. The following pages are about turning these ideas into finished songs.

It would be convenient if you could always write songs in a fixed order – if you could finish writing the words, then work out the rhythm, then write a melody and finally add the chords. At least you would have a single straightforward chain of events to work with. But as you do more songwriting, you will find that it hardly ever happens that way.

In reality you are more likely to move back and forth between the elements, refining them as you go. Once you start writing your tune, you may need to alter your lyrics. Or you may find that by altering the chords you completely change the feel of your song and have to go back and rewrite the tune. This is what gives songs their individuality, and is the reason why the many thousands of songs you have ever heard all sound different to each other.

The songs

The following pages trace the development of the songs on the CD from idea to finished product. They look at how each song began, and how it was developed. There are also activities that help you to use some of the rhythms, chords and melodies as the basis for your own songs. This will show you some techniques for working with the ideas you generate, though it is no substitute for working through this process with your own songs. You can also see what would have happened to the songs if different decisions had been made at various stages.

If you used the list on page 7 to choose where to start, you could keep following that route on the next pages too. So if, for example, you began with the "Words" section because you liked *Something to believe in*, it could help to go to that song first in the next section because it follows the development of lyrics into a complete song. But you might find it just as useful to go to one of the other songs and follow its development, particularly if you are now feeling more comfortable with generating your own ideas.

When you come to the group of pages about each song, listen to the CD to remind yourself how it sounds. The pages tell you how the song was written, pointing out important features and anything unusual. They also contain suggestions about changing or rewriting a particular aspect of the song. Try as many of these as you can – writing, singing or playing. You will be surprised at how much difference even small changes make.

The "Different choices" sections contain alternative versions of the songs which show how they might have developed if the writer had followed another route.

Melody:
Something to believe in: p.41
Too much fun: p.53

Tune:
I can't live without you: p.38
You tore out my heart: p.50

Chords:
Baby my heart: p.47

Rhythm:
Boyfriend: p.35
Get your groove on: p.56

Texture:
You take me away: p.44

Starting with a rhythm: *Boyfriend*

Boyfriend began with a very simple rhythmic idea and developed from there into a straightforward, contemporary pop song that would probably be sung by a teenage girl.

Rhythm

The rhythmic style is clear from the outset. Look at the blocks or the standard notation below and listen to it on track 27 of the CD:

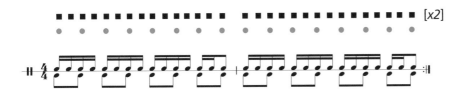

And this rhythm generated another rhythm that later became the vocal line:

And in music notation:

The bracket indicates the rhythm that became the hook – and the title of the song.

• Use the rhythm on track 27 as the basis for a new rhythm. Write your new rhythm down, then use it as the basis for some new lyrics.

Lyrics

The words "Boyfriend, my boyfriend" arose directly from the rhythm on track 28. These words suggested a tune which felt like a memorable hook (track 29) and formed the basis of the entire song.

At this point, it was necessary to decide what kind of song it was going to be. The simple repetition of the word "Boyfriend" had something yearning about it, which suggested that the song would be sung by someone looking from a distance at someone who is out of reach. So she sings "You ought to be mine", not "You are mine". The singer pretends that her out-of-reach fantasy boyfriend can hear all she's singing. She's probably in her room, imagining what it might be like to have him as her boyfriend. You can see the lyrics to the first verse of *Boyfriend* on page 11.

If you find it hard to decide what your song should say and who would sing it, try imagining a video for it. This will give you a story and a character.

• Of course the lyrics could take a different direction. You might hear something quite threatening in the hook on track 29. If so, try writing a "you've been cheating on me and I'm going to chuck you" lyric. Or you might hear something sarcastic in the hook – in which case write a "you want to be my boyfriend but you don't have a hope" lyric. Sing it to the tune of the verse (use track 30).

Boyfriend lyrics • melody • chords

The scheme of the lyrics is quite simple. The verse is in two halves:

> *I've been watchin' you for so, so long,*
> *Boyfriend, my boyfriend.*
> *You got the looks and you got it goin' on,*
> *Boyfriend, my boyfriend.*
>
> *Baby love I can't take it no longer*
> *You ought to be mine*
> *And I just won't hold it back no more*
> *Yes I want you by my side*

Unusually, the hook is in the verse, at the beginning of the song. It is repeated in lines one and three. The rhyme-scheme is ABAB.

"Mine" and "side" are half-rhymes. The change to ABCB gives this second half movement towards the chorus.

The chorus is just four lines:

> *Oops, ooh, baby though you're driving me crazy*
> *It's alright, it's alright*
> *Oh, you ignore me, I just won't let you*
> *Out my sight, out my sight*

The rhyme scheme here is ABCB, the same as the second half of the verse.

• Try writing another four lines for the chorus. What effect does lengthening the chorus have? Does it still sound as effective?

Melody

Boyfriend is quite downbeat, full of regret that the boyfriend isn't real. This is expressed in the first part of the verse by a melody that uses only a small number of notes. The hook, turning downwards on the syllable "friend", seems to express the singer's frustration.

What happens if you rewrite the melody using more notes, or changing the lengths of the gaps between the notes?

1. I've been watch-in' you for so, so long, boy-friend, my boy-friend.

You got the looks and you got it go-in' on, boy-friend, my boy-friend.

Can you write a different version of the hook that goes up at the end? What's the effect?

The second section of the verse melody is higher, and builds into the chorus. The chorus (track 31) is even higher, but it still ends back at the first note of the verse – the singer is getting nowhere.

Chords

The first four lines of the verse use only one chord, **Cm**, which makes this part of the song sound brooding and troubled. As the intensity increases at line 5, the chord changes to **Fm**, but the big chord change is at line 7, where **D** and **G** lead into the chorus. But even in the chorus the chords are rooted to the spot, going over the same ground without getting anywhere. These chords feature a common pop device – one chord to the bass note of another – in this case **G7** with a D bass and **Cm** with an Eb bass. Although it's animated, it still sinks back to the original **Cm** chord for the next verse.

Using just one chord builds tension because listeners usually expect faster chord changes. Do it Again by Steely Dan uses this effect very cleverly.

What would happen if you substituted C major for C minor and altered the melody to match? Would the song sound different?

Boyfriend chords • arrangement

Because the lyric is about someone getting nowhere, the chords and melody don't really move – they sound static and stuck. Even the middle section – the bridge – goes back to the opening percussion with the singer whispering the words "wanting" "waiting" "needing" "waking" – all words designed to emphasise her isolation.

20

Madonna's Justify my love *also uses this device.*

Arrangement

The instrumentation of this song is quite simple – just drums and sequenced keyboards. This has the effect of allowing the voice to tell its story without distracting the listener too much. But we know from the beginning that the singer is agitated and excited, partly because of the distinctive texture of the accompaniment.

What effect would a slower, less jagged accompaniment have?

32

In U2's Where the streets have no name, *the calm opening gives way to a rapid texture, creating a sense of mysterious anxiety.*

Different choices

On track 33 you can hear a rough arrangement of a different version of *Boyfriend*. It uses the same rhythm, but the notes are different. The verse line has slightly wider leaps, and it goes down then up.

33

Because the chords change much more quickly than they do in the original version, the whole thing is much less tense. And because it is in a major key rather than the minor, the atmosphere is less brooding. And instead of the rapid, trembling accompaniment, there are some jaunty percussion chords.

The result sounds much happier than the original. Would the existing lyrics still work just as well? Or would this new, slightly cheeky version be better with happier lyrics? Get writing . . .

Going further

Think of a frustrating situation and write some lyrics about it. How would you express that frustration with a melody, with chords and with a song structure?

Can you think of accompaniment textures that could express anxiety? And those that express relaxation? What makes one different from the other?

Not all rapid textures sound anxious. Listen to Robert Palmer's Woke up laughing.

I can't live without you began with the melody of the chorus, which just came into my head one day:

(34)

This is a positive, major key melody. The first note of the tune turns out to be the highest, which gives it a very strong feeling right from the start. The first words – "I can't live" – are punched out on the beat. The rest of the phrase sounds a bit more conversational, but the melody still leads back to the same three accented notes – "day I think" – so the key words get the most prominent notes.

The first three notes are definitely the hook in this song. What happens if you sing E, D, D instead of E, E, D? Is it as effective?

This simple, heartfelt chorus is followed by an equally heart-on-sleeve verse. It starts tenderly:

(35)

The simple repetitive phrases use the same few notes. This conversational style makes it seem as though the singer is speaking directly to the listener. The second half of the verse goes higher than ever and is capped by a swoop up to a high A, where the depth of feeling is matched by the height of the melody:

(36)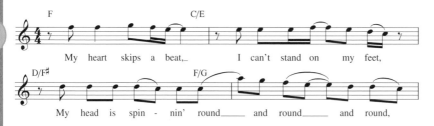

Drawing a graph of a melody

Draw a graph that shows how the melody of *I can't live without you* rises and falls. Use any notation you like – either something like the graph on page 8 or the one on page 50. This will show you high and low points of the tune and how these form patterns – it is often easier to see these than it is to hear them.

You can do this with any song you know. Look out for common patterns. For example, in many songs the melody reaches a peak only a few times (often near the end).

Write a new melody that follows the contours of the graph you have drawn.

I can't live without you lyrics • chords

From the outset the melody suggested a song that would be sung by a boy band. Like many songs of this type, it begins with the chorus. The first words came almost at the same time as the tune:

I can't live without ya,
Baby, you're the one, I just want you to know.
Every night and day I think about ya,
Stay forever mine, 'cause I can't let you go.

Say these words and try to find the places for the stresses, as you did on page 11. You will find that you are forced to put the main stresses on "I can't live" in line 1 then "one" and "know" in line 2. Where would you put the stresses in lines 3 and 4?

Experiment with putting the stresses in different places. You may well end up with a different version.

The format of the song is: Introduction (with some vocal ad libs), chorus, verse 1, chorus, verse 2, chorus, bridge, choruses to fade. The bridge gives a short contrast before the final choruses. It doesn't rhyme – it's more a collection of catchy, rhythmic phrases leading back to the familiar melody. Their unpredictability makes the predictability of the chorus words all the more appealing.

You're my angel, ooh.
You're my lady, a very special lady.
You're my comfort, a shoulder I can lean on
Anytime that I can't face the world.

Try writing lyrics in this format for a boy- or girl-band. Use a simple idea, with lots of repetition, then add a short contrasting bridge section.

Chords
The chords to this song are very simple, particularly in the chorus. The effect is straightforward and "from the heart".

What happens if you change the order of these chords? Play C, F, Dm7, C on guitar or keyboard and sing the melody. Which version do you prefer?

The verse chords are shown in the examples opposite. They move away from the tonic key, as the melody is more complex. Some of them have altered bass notes – for example *C/E* is a C major chord with E in the bass. Chord voicings like this create an instability that leads back to the simple chorus.

The chords in the bridge (track 38) are different. The relative minor, *Am*, makes its first appearance, although it is quickly countered by chords of *F* and *C*. At the end of the bridge are the two bars shown below. The chords *Gsus G* pull us back to the chorus:

37

27

38

I can't live without you   chords • rhythm • arrangement

Adding chords to an existing melody

Sing the tune of *I can't live without you* and, on guitar or keyboard, find other chords that work with it. (The song is in the key of C, so start by using the chords closest to that key: **F, G, Dm, Am, Em.**) It may take a few tries to get something you like. The more you do this – and you can do it with any song you know – the more familiar you will become with how notes and chords fit together. You may not improve the original, but the point is to begin combining chords yourself to get a feel for what you like and what you don't. This is a good way to stimulate your own ideas for songs.

Try substituting D major for D minor in the second bar. Which do you prefer?

27

Rhythm

The underlying rhythm of this song is a simple eight quavers to a bar. But there is an additional rhythmic feature: a "push" (an accent before the beat) which happens frequently in the introduction and the chorus. This gives the song a slight sense of urgency.

In Long Distance Love by Little Feat, pushes create a sense of uncertainty. Listen to Monkey Wrench by the Foo Fighters, too.

To hear this without the pushes, move the last chords of bars 1 and 3 on to the first beat of the next bar.

39

Arrangement

The backing for this is a standard band of keyboard, guitar, bass and drums with some "sweetening" from strings. However, the song itself is the centre of attention and therefore the piece is not really dependent on a particular instrumentation – just guitar or piano alone would create much the same effect as the band.

Different choices

On track 40 is a version of the song that has exactly the same melody but different chords. By using minor chords instead of the major chords in the original, a more melancholy effect is created.

40

Going further

Write a song that is so driven by its melody that it doesn't need an accompaniment. Keep it very simple at first, with plenty of repetition. If you write a strong enough melody, you should be able to sing it unaccompanied and it will still make sense to the listener. A tune that is this effective without accompaniment will be the basis of a really convincing song when fully arranged.

Many show tunes are very strong melodically. Stephen Sondheim's Sorry Grateful, from the show Company, is a good example.

Starting with a lyric: *Something to believe in*

03

Something to believe in started with images of unpleasant things –
cold wind, storms, unpaid bills and so on. As I pieced these together
I felt I wanted to write a song reassuring the listener that the singer
was someone they could depend on and believe in. So the words of
the verse describe bad situations, but already offer hope:

> **When the cold wind blows and the lightning strikes,**
> **If you're on your own, it's been a long, hard fight.**
> **It's nothing new, but it's strong and true**
> **You can depend on . . .**

The second half of the verse has the same structure:

> **If you've just got tired and the gas bill's come,**
> **Control seems lost, never felt so low,**
> **It's nothing new, but it's strong and true**
> **You can depend on . . .**

I was happy with these verse lyrics but felt I didn't have anything to
add for a chorus. So I simply re-used the verse words for the chorus,
changing the music to make the message louder and clearer and
inserting the hook "something to believe in". Verse 2 has a similar
structure to verse 1, but the words are getting more hopeful. And
again, they are repeated in the chorus with the hook added.

*Try this yourself – write the
lyrics of a verse and then
use them for the chorus,
changing the music only.
If you have a phrase that
sums up the song, add it to
the chorus as an extra line.*

> **You say you need a friend, there's no need to ask;**
> **I'll be on your side with the hardest task.**
> **It's nothing new, but it's strong and true**
> **You can rely on . . .**
> **Oh, hope is never lost and life ain't really blue;**
> **The time has come to live, let courage see you through**
> **It's nothing new , it's strong and true**
> **You can rely on . . .**

Rhythm

With lyrics this strong and definite, a rhythmic pattern suggested
itself very quickly. I read the words through and chose the ones that
I felt were most important, and this was where I placed the stresses.
There are many different ways of doing this with these lyrics – I
went for a pattern that sounded very solid and straightforward,
which I then repeated a number of times throughout the verse.
Here it is as blocks and as music:

11

Something to believe in   rhythm • melody • chords

42

But the same words suggested a completely different rhythm for the chorus – proving that many rhythms will work for most sets of words, and that each rhythm will give the words a new character.

[x2]

Turning lyrics into a rhythm

If you already have a set of lyrics that you can use as both verse and chorus, try using them as the basis for two different rhythms. One could be fast, the other slow. You might also find that by stressing different words you bring out different meanings.

Melody

43

As I worked on the rhythms – particularly on making contrasts between the one for the verse and the one for the chorus – fragments of melody began to emerge. The melody of the verse looks like this:

This is a positive melody, with a definite, confident shape and a clear structure which is then repeated for the second part of the verse. It starts with a leap upwards as though attracting attention, then leaps all the way down again from an even higher note. The melody then steps calmly down to the final phrase "you can depend on". The singer is someone who can cope in a crisis! The chorus melody is more dramatic, higher in pitch and is obviously trying to be very persuasive.

Chords

The melody – particularly the verse – seemed to require strong, positive chords with a sense of direction. Here they are:

44

This is a good principle for songwriting – find a chord progression you can use for the introduction and for the verse, but use different rhythms and textures for each section.

These chords are used in different ways in the song – both for the piano introduction and the electric guitar part in the verse.

Something to believe in   chords • arrangment

The only other chords used are the chorus chords, which are quite different in effect from the verse – more rock-influenced:

Arrangement

Because there is little difference lyrically between the verse and the chorus in this song, the contrast has to be created in other ways. So the finished recording has plenty of changing textures and a variety of instrumental moods. Here is a plan of the different sections:

• The introduction is very clear and bright, with a distinctive combination of piano, organ and banjo. The piano plays a gentle figure which suggests a nursery rhyme.

• This gives way to the denser sound of the verse, which is dominated by electric guitar. The accompaniment rhythms are more jagged and energetic, building towards the chorus.

• The chorus is denser still, with a particularly big drum sound. The tone of the singing changes too, and is suddenly harsher and more emphatic.

• At the end of each chorus the introduction returns in a much shorter form: on the playout it is preceded by a dramatic stop.

Going further

Write a set of lyrics – four or eight lines is enough – and use them as the basis for as many different rhythms and melodies as you can. Can you write a melody to your lyrics that feels the exact opposite of what the words are trying to express?

The idea that the shape of a melody tells you something about the song – or even about the singer – may seem strange at first. Listen to the songs on the CD and think about the different melodic styles. Do large leaps in melodies feel different from small steps? How do they affect the character of the song?

Different choices

On track 46 there is an altered version of the melody. Listen to it a few times and sing both versions. Here's the first line written down:

Can you describe the difference? It isn't huge, but it is definitely there. The new version feels less confident. Make small changes to your own melodies and describe their effects. This will help you to write more expressive tunes that reflect the emotions in your lyrics.

Starting with a texture: *You take me away*

04

You take me away was inspired by a combination of sounds heard one day in the studio while arranging some other music. The texture – acoustic guitar with a touch of percussion, punctuated by small silences – was so distinctive that it very quickly suggested ways of using it. Rhythm and chords came almost at the same time. This is what the guitar plays at the beginning:

Listen carefully to the opening of the song. Can you identify the percussion instrument in the opening bars? What happens in bars three and four?

47

Rhythm

The guitar figure is syncopated (accents come in parts of the bar where you don't expect them) with lots of pushes (accented notes before the beat). Here's a simple version of it (blocks and music notation). This is the basic rhythm of the entire song. Tap the top line with two fingers of your right hand and the bottom line with your left hand.

48

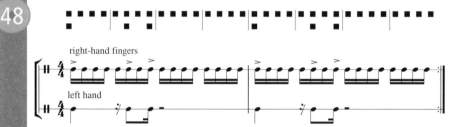

Get someone else to play the guitar figure while you play the percussion parts – it will take a bit of practice!

Chords

You take me away uses more complex chords than many pop songs, partly because it is trying to express complex emotions. We have already looked at the basic progression on page 26, but it is useful to examine it in a bit more detail here. Here are the chords to the first part of the verse:

49

Dm9 has an expressive, yearning quality. **F2** is a major chord in which the 2nd (G in a chord of F) has been substituted for the more usual 3rd (A in a chord of F). This sequence helps to create tension and release, but it also feels as if it isn't going anywhere – it seems to spiral around on itself, always leading back to the start. These chords are repeated four times in the first part of the verse, building up tension both through repetition and also through the character of the chords used. We still haven't heard the tonic or "home" chord yet, so everything still feels unresolved.

Build some "ambiguous" sequences of your own by trying out complex chords on keyboard or guitar. Alternating complex and simple chords can create an interesting effect.

In the second part of the verse, some more straightforward chords make it seem as if some kind of resolution might be approaching:

5

F   **G**   **Am**   [*x3*]
Dm7   **Esus7**   **E**

A "sus" chord is a major chord where the 3rd of the chord (G♯ in a chord of E) is raised by a semitone (A in a chord of E).

So the verse chords start from the two-bar guitar figure, but bit by bit they become less mysterious and more positive. By the time it reaches the end, the verse is moving somewhere. In the chorus, the chords feel much more certain and happy. It almost feels as if the sun has come out. And we finally hear the tonic chord (**C**).

51

F   **G**   **C**   [*x4*]

Working with chords and their moods
You can grade chords according to their mood – tense, dark, menacing or happy, cheerful, outgoing and so on. Play the chords below, one at a time, or listen to them on track 52 of the CD. How would you describe each one?

52

Working through a series of chords like this, you can construct progressions that move through various feelings and moods. The emotional "graph" of a song can be plotted through chords and their relationships before you even think about a melody or lyric.

Lyrics
As we have seen, the character of the song was already there in the chord progression as it moved from anxiety to happiness. It wasn't hard to make the lyrics do the same thing. The words of the verse came in little bursts, partly influenced by the syncopated nature of the opening texture, particularly the gaps in it.

> *Lately*
> *I'm finding it hard to go to sleep*
> *I'm tossing and turning*
> *and it's making me feel weak*

The singer is so in love he can't sleep properly – the gaps make him sound nervous and distracted. But in the second half of the verse, where the chords become more positive and confident, the words flow more smoothly and continuously:

> *Oh what joy, when I speak your name,*
> *Feels so good inside.*
> *Oh the joy, when I see your face,*
> *I can't wait to make you, make you mine . . .*

a tumble of words as the singer wakes up properly
love (supported by those bright major chords):

..ke me away into the clouds where I'm in love.
.nen I'm in your arms I feel a special kind of love.
I never knew that I could have someone like you,
But like in a dream I know things really can come true.

Melody and structure

The melody flowed from the lyrics, starting low and subdued and
winding its way higher towards the chorus. If you draw a graph of
the melody you will see how it mirrors the emotions expressed in
the chords and words. The structure is fairly straightforward:

Can you spot the highest note in the song? Is it in the verse or the chorus? Or somewhere else?

**Intro • Verse 1 • Chorus • Intro • Verse 2 • Chorus •
Bridge • Chorus • Intro (fade to end)**

The bridge section expresses doubt again ("Friends they say I'm
crazy for believing") with the chords of **Esus**, **E** and **Am** turning
away from the major chords of the chorus. But in spite of this the
melody climbs even higher than before, as though dispelling all
remaining doubts before the final chorus.

Arrangement

There is a gradual build-up of texture at the beginning – starting
with just guitar and triangle, then (after a sweep of harp strings)
adding bass and drums to build into the verse. But the arrangement
is actually very simple. It provides a backdrop – the anxious rhythm
at the beginning and the lush backing vocals for the chorus, for
example – but it doesn't overpower the solo singer, who is the
main focus of attention.

Different choices

On track 54 of the CD you can hear the opening of *You take me
away* played on different instruments. Can you tell what they are?
And can you hear how the effect changes? Somehow the sense of
urgency is missing. And of course, because this figure repeats
throughout the song, changing the instrument would alter its
mood completely. Somehow the steel-strung acoustic guitar I used
does give the song just the right amount of quiet intensity and yet
helps keep rhythmic momentum because of its percussive nature.

Going further

Start a song with a repeated two-bar progression, then develop it in
various ways. Can you make your chords move through different
emotions? When you have a progression you are happy with, add
lyrics and melody.

Can you invent a distinctive texture to use as the basis for a song?
Think of some combinations of instruments and voices that work
well together and get a group of players together to try your ideas.

God only knows by the Beach Boys and Aqueous transmission by Incubus both use interesting instrumental textures.

Starting with a chord progression: *Baby my heart* (05)

Baby my heart started with a chord progression which I found while playing the keyboard one day:

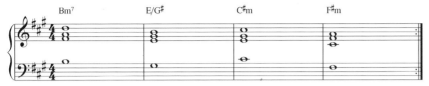

55

This sounded like it could be in either F♯ minor or in A major – it felt rather unsettled, which made me want to explore it more. So I played around with the chords and ended up with a slightly more unusual last chord:

A very good exercise is to play a chord progression like the one above in a number of keys – ideally all 12! Get used to the idea of chord relationships remaining constant whatever the key.

56

This has a more strongly emotional effect. The **C♯m** chords sinks darkly downwards to the **Bm7** chord – which is also the first chord of the progression, so there is a "loop" effect.

This felt like it could be the first half of a chorus. On the repeat of the sequence, I tried ending a bit more hopefully, substituting a **D** for the final chord:

57

These chords felt to me like the emotional core of the song and, whatever happened subsequently, I felt that they would be the centrepiece. I added chords for what felt like a verse and eventually chords for a middle section as well, but my initial chord idea still felt like the chorus – and so it proved:

58

This is a clear example of what happens when you "fine-tune" chord sequences – you find all sorts of different shades of feeling and emotion as you move through the different options.

Baby my heart lyrics • melody • structure

The singer of *Baby my heart* is saying things that are very charming but also rather superficial:

> **If you were mine, you'd be my lady forever.**
> **Sweeter than wine, I would love you more than treasure.**

Sweet-sounding words maybe, but not too profound. Many songs are like this – pretty enough on the surface but without many deep emotions. And sometimes songs like this are exactly what you want to hear – light, smooth and easy to listen to. But it can be difficult to write something that sounds completely effortless and simple.

Luther Vandross's Busy Body *may sound simple, but the arrangement and structure are complicated. Listen to* Cocoon *by Björk, too, or* Hard to Explain *by the Strokes – just how simple are they?*

Melody and structure

The chorus melody (see previous page) has only four notes, which makes it easy to remember and sing. Its simplicity sounds very heartfelt, almost pleading. It also makes the chords underneath seem richer and more expressive, creating tension between the sweetness of the tune and the slight bitterness of the harmonies.

The verse and the bridge use a wider range of notes than the chorus, which makes them feel as if genuine emotions are nearer the surface. The verse melody has two identical phrases:

Can you think of a different second phrase to answer the first one, instead of repeating it?

The singer is trying to create a polished effect, with the pretty rhymes and matching musical phrases. The final phrase swoops up into the chorus:

Baby my heart rhythm • arrangement

The structure of *Baby my heart* is like many pop songs:

Intro • Verse 1 • Chorus • Verse 2 • Chorus • Bridge • Chorus • Chorus

The final repetition of the chorus moves up a tone into the key of C♯ minor. This is a common technique at the end of a song, and it heightens the emotional effect – try it with a song of your own.

The last chorus of That other girl *(Burt Bacharach and Elvis Costello) moves down a tone – an unusual effect!*

Arrangement

The arrangement contributes to the song's momentum. In the introduction and choruses, strings add rich expression to the simple emotions. The verses are simpler, relying mainly on acoustic guitar, but here and there bell and piano sounds mirror the contours of the vocal line – this adds a delicate emphasis in significant places.

Picking out a particular vocal line by copying it in an instrumental part is a common but very effective arrangement technique.

The vocal arrangement – the combination of soloist and backing singers – is quite complex. In verse 1 there are no backing vocals at all, but in the chorus the backing voices carry the melody while the soloist's line sounds almost improvised. This adds the impression that the soloist is singing "from the heart" as he weaves his own line around the melody. The backing singers drop out again at the start of verse 2, but they accompany one or two key phrases ("Night after night"), heightening their impact.

Vocal arrangements are a subject in themselves. Any song by the Beach Boys will show how complicated vocal parts add depth to very simple songs.

All the different elements are used in different ways. For example the bridge is solo vocal (no backing), strings and bells, while in the last choruses the solo vocal is silent and the backing vocals lead the song to the end. The changes in texture, created from just a few different elements, add shape, contrast and dynamic.

A lot of soul and r&b music contains ornamented vocal lines. Fallin' *by Alicia Keys is a good example of this. Listen to Aretha Franklin, Bobby Womack, Mary J. Blige and R. Kelly as well.*

Take parts of this song – or a song of your own – to experiment with simple arrangements. Use either acoustic instruments or MIDI to add instruments and combine them to create expressive effects.

Even revoicing a chord on the guitar or keyboard and adding another vocal line is a "rearrangement" of your song.

Different choices

Track 61 is a new version of the verse and chorus with a different melody. Firstly, the contours are reversed – where the original goes up, the new version goes down, and so on. Can you describe the effect of this? The new chorus has a wider range of notes, making it more expressive but less "hooky". And one of the chorus chords has been changed to match one of the examples on page 47 – can you tell which one? Does this improve the harmony or not?

Going further

On track 62 you can hear the chords of the chorus of *Baby my heart* repeated in a loop. Sing different melodies over the top until you find one you like, then write it down. (You can use the same lyrics or make some up – you can alter the rhythm as much as you like.) Then use your new melody as the basis for a new song of your own.

Starting with a melody: *You tore out my heart*

06

You tore out my heart began with a few notes from an A minor scale.

63

This already has a sad, introspective quality. You can start with just a short row of notes, not even in a rhythm. Any group of notes has certain qualities, happy, sad, funny, mysterious and so on. Once the notes were there, I began to play with the rhythm of the melody and tried altering only the final note on the repeat:

Try creating a melody with no more than five notes (you can repeat them, of course) and see what sort of moods you can create.

64

The way the phrase curls round itself, then goes up, first by a small step in bar 2, then by a leap in bar 4 suggests deep feelings that are rising to the surface – an unfolding story.

How would you follow this? I felt that the height already reached (a full octave – or eight notes – above the starting note) meant that the melody was quite likely to climb down again, forming a shape rather like this:

When you start writing a melody, plotting a graph like this can help – even before you put any actual notes on paper. Graphs let you find interesting melodic shapes, and may help to find a melody that is stuck at the back of your mind.

Here's what I came up with as the "answer" to the initial "question":

Try writing different answering phrases to the opening four bars. There are always plenty of options!

65

At this point I felt that I had a verse, but that I wanted to repeat it to maximise the rather brooding, intense atmosphere. So the first section looks like this (complete with lyrics, which were already forming at this point):

66

It's cold and lone - ly once a - gain; Don't know if I can stand the pain.

I real - ly need - ed you, sup - pose that I still do the same.

I'm stand - ing by what I be - lieve. I can - not bring my - self to leave.

It seems to burn in - side, this feel - ing I can't hide. D'you see?

Can you use this melody as the basis for a set of lyrics of your own? Sing your lyrics over the top of the melody on track 66.

You tore out my heart   lyrics • structure • chords

The lyrics sprang directly from the feeling of the melody.
Imagining the video to the song, I see a singer describing a
situation that she has been in before ("it's cold and lonely once
again"). She's trying to decide whether to stay or go. The dark,
minor key indicates that she wants to leave, but the upward leaps
of the melody suggest something else besides. This is explained in
the chorus:

> *Every time I breathe I cannot believe*
> *We're still standing after all the years.*
> *All the hurt and pain I'd live through again*
> *By understanding why we both shed those tears*
> *But if it's time for us to drift apart*
> *There'd be just one thing that's on my mind –*
> *I've been wondering why you tore out my heart.*

Internal rhymes (breathe/believe, pain/again) help to create the
impression of strong feelings welling up again and again.

Structure
This song has one of the simplest structures in the book:

Verse 1 • Verse 2 • Chorus • Verse 3 • Chorus

It's quite a short song, too, because it's all about one particular
situation and there isn't a great deal of change of mood. The
singer is condemned to go over the same ground again and again.

Because the song is emotionally intense, it doesn't actually feel short. Long, intense songs – like Jimmy Webb's McArthur Park – can be quite difficult to listen to.

67

Chords
The opening piano figure sets the scene immediately – a minor 9th
chord with a yearning, plaintive sound:

This texture is often used at the start of ballads. You can hear it in Eternal Flame by the Bangles and Going Back by Dusty Springfield.

The tension of the minor chord keeps "resolving" to the more
neutral sound of **F2** (an F major chord where the A is replaced by
a G). This seems to express the idea that the singer feels full of
tension, but keeps trying to accept the situation as well.

You tore out my heart   chords • arrangement • rhythm

68

The chorus chords seem to brighten the mood, starting in C major, but they change very quickly. It feels as if the singer is accepting defeat and moving on with the words "But if it's time for us to drift apart". But then there is a gap in the melody, during which the singer seems to contemplate the idea. After this, the bitter last line leads back into the despairing minor chords of the verse.

Play these chords over a few times to hear how quickly their mood changes.

The piano figure in bars 3 and 4 of this line prepares us for the final phrase of the chorus and makes it stand out more.

Arrangement and rhythm
The song works well with piano alone, and this is how the recording begins. The style doesn't really demand any rhythmic accompaniment at all. Verses 1 and 2 are underlaid with a few string chords. In the chorus, bass, drums and electric guitar add weight and intensity. The rhythm section stays in for verse 3 (snare-drum is added too, so the whole arrangement builds into the second chorus. But at the repeat of the last line, the instruments drop out, leaving the singer alone once again.

Emotional songs don't always need an intense arrangement. Compare Whitney Houston's version of I will always love you with the original recording by Dolly Parton. Which is more powerful?

Different choices
69

On track 69 there is a version of the melody without the leaps. You can hear how much less expressive and tense it feels. The shape of a melody can have a very dramatic effect on the emotional tone of a piece. If you want to express more extreme emotions, you often need to have wider leaps in the vocal line.

Extreme leaps can express very strong emotions and loss of control. Listen to My Way by Frank Sinatra or Big Time Sensuality by Björk for examples of this.

Experiment with "extreme" vocal leaps to express more extreme emotions. Take one of your existing tunes and "stretch" the intervals (gaps between the notes). How far can you push it?

Going further
Try expressing hopefulness, resignation, anger or frustration in a song. Of course you can do this through lyrics, but you have to get the music to match. Would you do this mostly through the melody, or do you think chords are better? And what about the arrangement? Do certain instruments express certain emotions?

Stevie Wonder's Living for the city expresses many of these emotions at once by combining several different melodic, harmonic and instrumental features.

Starting with a lyric: *Too much fun*

07

Too much fun began life with that phrase. While talking about a particularly dangerous activity, a friend said "That sounds like too much fun". Someone else said "You can't have too much fun!" And I took it from there. Most of the lyrics were written before any of the music. But it was clear from an early stage that the phrase would make a good hook-line. It very quickly became:

If you carry a notebook with you, you can make a note of any interesting phrases that you hear in conversation for use in songs later!

> **Well, that's too much fun, I said that's too much fun.**
> **I said that's too much fun for me to be having tonight.**

Each verse contains a series of ideas leading into these two lines. I wanted each one to sound more ridiculous than the last. Verse 1:

If you think of a short, catchy phrase, see how many times you can get away with repeating it! A strong hook can result almost immediately.

> **Well he's a smooth operator, he said "I'll see you later,**
> **We'll all go into town and drink a case of tequila"**
> **Well, that's too much fun, I said that's too much fun.**
> **I said that's too much fun for me to be having tonight.**

The idea of drinking not a glass of tequila but a case of it makes the idea of fun seem both ridiculous and dangerous, and therefore not much fun at all. The internal rhyme ("operator/later") adds to this sense of the ridiculous. The next verses continue in this way:

> **He phones up my sister, the sneaky little twister**
> **He's got a bad reputation for over-complication**

The verse lyrics, full of jokey rhymes and tongue-twisters, create a picture of a fast talker, a player with words. By contrast the chorus contains one simple repeated idea, which gives it real swagger.

Chords

The lyrics suggested a straightforward rock-and-roll tune. I began playing with a 12-bar blues progression, trying to work out where the phrase "too much fun" would fit (and where it wouldn't). Try this for yourself. Listen to the blues progression on track 70 and try singing the title phrase at various points. Where does it fit best?

My solution was to fit the phrase over the chords printed in orange on the chart below. Listen to track 70 again (or play the chords on guitar or keyboard), and sing the title phrase at these points.

A	A	A	A
D	D	A	A
E	D	A	A

In the song itself, I substituted the chords **G** and **D** (two beats each) for the **D** in the third line. This gives the progression more power and variety while still being a basic 12-bar blues.

Try substitutions in your own progressions. Change chords one by one until you find a combination you like.

Rhythm

I knew I wanted the song to have a rock accompaniment like the one on track 71. The rhythm of the vocal line fell into place over the top of this. Play this, and try saying the words of verse 1 over the top. There are many ways of making them fit. My solution for the first two lines was:

Use this accompaniment as the basis for your own lyrics – just make them up over the top. This can be a good way of getting new ideas for a song.

Try tapping the rhythm while playing the accompaniment.

Melody

The final melody, built up from the rhythm above, is full of major and minor thirds ("blue" notes):

Try creating your own melodies using the example as a guide for which notes to try over the chords of Too much fun.

Structure

When I played all three verses one after the other, it seemed a bit boring. This is partly because there is no chorus in a blues structure like this. Verses 1 and 2 together seemed fine, but after that I knew I needed to add a bridge section for variety and extra interest.

20

So far, the song was written from my point of view: me looking at the hero (or villain). In the bridge, he puts his own point of view. The harmonies move up a fourth, which seems to make it sound like someone else's voice. The chords, which are shown over the top of the lyrics, are slightly more adventurous than those in the verses:

> **D**
> *He says "there's no such thing as too much fun,*
> **A**
> *People been havin' it since time begun.*
> **D**
> *One more ride on a carousel*
> **A**
> *Never sent nobody down to hell!"*
> **D**
> *I said "Gimme a break, I want to stay alive,*
> **A**　　　　　　　　　　　　　**F♯7**
> *I'm tryin' to hold down my nine to five.*
> **Bm**　　　　　　　　**E7**　　　**A**
> *You'll never catch me havin' – too much fun."*

Verse 3 then followed, but the song still seemed too short. Time for that classic rock device – a guitar solo. Because it uses the verse chords, the solo feels like a verse in the overall structure, but gives the listener a break from all the wordiness. The guitar is the ideal instrument, because it sounds as rebellious as the subject of the song. In the end I decided to put the solo before verse three. But it still felt as though I needed the bridge again to come out of the verse – this time I gave it different words.

The long coda (end section) and fade-out seem to suggest that no-one will ever change this man's behaviour, so it's best to let him disappear over the horizon. The structure of the song is:

Introduction • Verse 1 • Verse 2 • Bridge •
Guitar solo (over verse) • Verse 3 • Bridge • Coda

This is a rather different structure from the other songs in the book, as it doesn't really have a well-defined chorus. Instead it uses a single phrase which recurs at the end of each blues verse as a hook.

Arrangement
The backing is for a standard large rock-and-roll band: electric guitar, honky-tonk piano, organ, bass and drums. There is a brass section of trumpet and two saxophones too. Everyone plays the opening three notes – a sort of call to attention! The verse is accompanied by rhythm section, with simple, chugging guitar chords and blues figures on piano. The chorus has hammered piano quavers and backing vocals as well as organ.

Different choices
If you replace the expression "too much fun" with a different phrase, you change the mood immediately. Somehow the slightly sarcastic, threatening atmosphere of the original disappears. It's just not as funny. Try saying the words of verse 1 with this replacement lyric, and listen to it on track 75:

> *Well he's a smooth operator, he said "I'll see you later,*
> *We'll all go to town and drink a case of tequila"*
> *Well, that sounds good, I said that sounds good.*
> *I said that sounds good for me to be doing tonight.*

Going further
Think of a number of short phrases that might work as the hook of a song. Start up a simple rhythm, using just one chord at first, and see where the phrase fits best – and how many repetitions you can squeeze in! Then add in a few more chords – 12-bar blues is certainly worth a try – to form a complete verse. Then develop this into a song without a chorus using the structure outlined above.

How many songs can you think of that use a very short phrase – words or music – as a hook?

Too much fun is in many ways a standard guitar rock song. Groups like Status Quo perform similar blues-based music.

Many songs based on blues chords use a repeated phrase instead of an actual chorus: Oh boy! by Buddy Holly, One more bottle of wine by Emmylou Harris and Randy Newman's I think it's gonna rain today are good examples.

75

Try your own replacement phrase for "too much fun" and see what effects you can create.

Some suggestions for hook phrases: "Give it up," "I'm the one," "Think twice"

(76)

The starting point for *Get your groove on* was its "cut up", almost disjointed rhythmic style. It began with the bass drum pattern below. Tap the 4/4 beat with one hand and the bass drum part with your foot, so that you get a feeling for how physical it is:

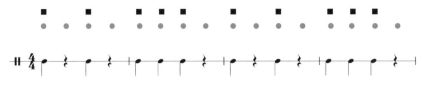

(77)

The next rhythm added was the hi-hat part. Tap it with one hand, with the same bass drum rhythm as above in your foot:

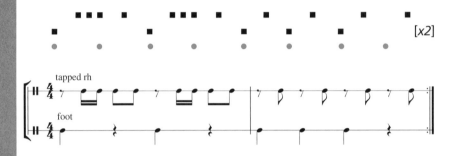

If you're really brave, tap the crotchet beat with your left hand, the hi-hat part with your right, and the bass drum part with your foot! The overall effect is slightly rigid – and the second bar of the bass drum sounds a bit like a march or a tango. But the cut up, gappy snare part adds a contemporary, swaggering feel.

(78)

Can you play hi-hat, snare and bass drum parts with hands and feet?

Play a very simple rhythm on a bass drum (if you can find one) or a cardboard box or table. See if a melody idea springs from this one rhythm. Even a simple 4/4 bass-drum figure can be enough to start you off. If nothing comes to mind, add in another percussion part to get the ideas flowing.

Then move on to more complicated rhythms. Use a drum machine or keyboard, or experiment with what you find around you. Ask other percussionists to join in – you'll be surprised at how intricate your rhythms can become. Use these as the basis for new songs.

Paul Simon's album Rhythm of the Saints *was inspired by South American drum music.*

Get your groove on lyrics • melody

Lyrics

The lyrics of "Get your groove on" aren't very profound – they are an invitation to dance! This song is to be chanted on the dancefloor or sung by a boy-band. Unusually, it starts with a chorus, so we are left in no doubt that we are straight into party mode. Everything, from the introduction, is designed to have little hooks that embed themselves in your mind and feet.

> **You can get your groove on in the house tonight;**
> **When you get your groove on you will feel alright.**
> **We can dance and party till the morning light;**
> **Get your groove on, groove on.**

The verses are really just expansions of the chorus, although with a different rhyme scheme:

> **If you wanna shake the party,**
> **If you wanna rock the floor,**
> **Let's get jiggy, let's get freaky,**
> **They'll be beggin' us for more.**

The bridge is just a short contrast section:

> **Relax and unwind, let me soothe your mind.**
> **Let's kick it tonight, it's so outta sight**
> **And I can't get enough.**

Words like "groove" and "jiggy" may feel old-fashioned to you. Think of some words you might use instead. Turn these into lyrics using short phrases and simple rhymes.

Melody

Like a lot of dance music, the melody of "Get your groove on" uses only a few notes. Here they are:

The simple, uncomplicated message of the song is reflected in the restricted range and the simplicity of the tune. The main focus is the chorus:

The melody of the verse is not that different from the chorus, except it doesn't have the distinctive three beats in the second bar. It is also restricted to even fewer notes, which makes the chorus even more the song's dominant feature.

Chords and structure

27

The chords of "Get your groove on" are simple, but their voicings are quite distinctive. Play them on a keyboard to get the full effect:

81

The verse contains slightly more complex chords: **A7♭9** (made up of A, C sharp, E, G, and B flat), **Dm9** (D, F, A, C, E) and **E7♯5** (E, G♯, C, D) These give a richer, yearning quality to the verse, but also create a sense of relief when we get back to the simpler chorus chords. The structure is simple, making the chorus the focus of attention:

Contrasting simple chorus chords with complex verse chords is a good way of creating tension and resolution in a song.

Chorus • Verse 1 • Chorus • Verse 2 • Chorus • Bridge • Chorus (fade)

Arrangement

Obviously the drum parts are very important in this dance tune, as is a synthesized bass. The rest of the texture is made up of samples (digitally operated recordings) of real instruments – acoustic guitar, strings and harpsichord. There are also "orchestral stabs" – samples of an entire orchestra playing a large chord – which add a slightly spiky, edgy feel. The instrumentation has a slightly classical feel. This is a common device in r&b and hip-hop.

Going further

If you take part of a classical tune and add the percussion parts from the foot of page 56, you give an instant hip-hop or r&b twist to the original piece. Here are the chords from the Canon by Pachelbel, written in the 17th century. What happens when you add a dance rhythm?

82

Think of styles that can be combined – rap and Latin, disco and classical – and combine the rhythmic style of one with the instrumentation of the other. Try playing a song on the "wrong" instruments to hear the effect – it might inspire you (or it might make you laugh).

Different choices

83

Track 83 shows what happens when you make a different choice right at the outset by changing the time signature to 3/4. It uses exactly the same chords as *Get your groove on* and the same melody. It comes from exactly the same place, but it sounds completely new. How far can you go to make one song into another? Can you think of lyrics for this new version?

What next?

Performing and publishing

Now you have written some songs and made some demos of them, how do you get other people to hear your work? The first thing to do is to ask friends and relatives to listen to your songs – either perform live, or play your demos. You can be sure of some instant feedback – and you may find out who your real friends are! (But bear in mind that people who are close to you may be a bit biased.)

The next stage might be to try to find someone else to play your songs with – perhaps another guitarist if you play guitar, or a singer if you're a piano player. With these small combinations you can experiment with harmony vocals and other aspects of arrangement. Sometimes your songs change as you perform them with different musicians or combinations of instruments – this can be very exciting and give you inspiration for your future writing.

For some styles, you need more players. You may want to form a band to play your material. The practical side of running a band – finding a place to rehearse, getting enough equipment together and organising rehearsals – is difficult enough before you even think about the music. But nothing equals the feeling of playing your songs in public. You learn what works and what doesn't from your audience, and this helps your songwriting. (And sometimes you will find that the musicians you have don't suit the songs. You have two choices – change the band or write different songs!)

Being in a band takes a lot of energy and commitment. But when it works, it is worth all the effort.

Some styles, particularly styles like *Boyfriend* and *Get your groove on*, depend more on computerised recording (sequencing). You can buy software and a microphone for a home computer, or you may know someone with a computer music set-up (or even a studio of some kind) who would let you create a demo of your song. This is another fascinating way of spending days and days of your life. It also gives you the opportunity to make several different versions of your songs – this can be useful when deciding what works best.

If you enjoy the technology aspect of making music, you might prefer working this way to playing in a band. Recording can be just as interesting as playing live.

This might be enough for you – to write, record and perform to a local audience. But many writers dream of the fame and fortune achieved by the biggest stars. This is the hard part. Companies who might be interested in your songs have to be persuaded to listen to them, either live or on a recording. The live method is to play in public as often as possible, build up a following and eventually hire a manager to act on your behalf, contacting record companies, booking concerts, organising publicity and so on. This route has worked for countless musicians. But make sure your manager is someone you can trust, who will work hard for your success.

For recordings, you need to send your demo directly to producers, agents, managers and publishers. These people receive thousands of tapes each year, so you have to compete to be noticed. Most record companies have a department called A&R (artists and repertoire) – this is usually a good place to start.

You may not want to perform your songs – many songwriters only write for other performers. If you have a particular artist in mind, find out who that person's management company is and send a demo there. But again, remember you will be one of many.

You will have heard your own songs over and over again, but the people who receive your demo will be hearing it for the first time. Be as creative as you were when you wrote the songs! Here are a few tips for getting your work noticed:

• Don't make your intro too long – get to the best part of the song quickly. If it's the chorus, start with the chorus!

• Don't send too many songs at once. Three is usually enough. If the person listening is interested, they will contact you for more.

• Make the most of what you can do – as well as a demo of the music, you might want to send pictures or a video of yourself. But make everything you send as professional as possible.

• Once you have sent your tapes, wait. Give people time to react. Don't pester them – it doesn't work.

• Don't send the only copy of your work – it may not come back.

There is also a lot of information on the internet about promoting your own songs and there are websites where you can upload your demos. This can be a very useful way of getting your work heard – and record companies do visit these sites to find interesting new writers – but beware of copyright implications. Before you decide to put your songs on an internet site, look carefully at the terms and conditions. Make sure the song remains your copyright and see what provisions the site itself makes for protecting this.

The internet can be a good way of meeting musicians with similar tastes to yours. You can even collaborate online, playing and recording with musicians all over the world.

61

A record company is unlikely to use your work in the form that you send it. They will want changes. It is up to you whether you follow their advice. They often know what works commercially, while you may feel reluctant to alter your writing. But if someone takes the trouble to make these suggestions, it is because they feel that your work has potential. So it could be worth compromising.

If you are really talented, it is likely that someone will notice your songs. If this happens, you will have started on the long journey to making a name – perhaps even a living – as a songwriter. It takes effort, determination and luck, and if you want huge commercial success you must be prepared to work very hard to earn it.

Protecting yourself – and others

Here is some basic advice about the legal implications of sending your work to a performer, agent or publisher, and also about what happens if you are successful in selling your songs. Copyright – ownership of ideas – is a complex area of law, so if you are offered a contract, make sure you take plenty of advice before you sign.

Firstly, before you send your songs away, you need to be sure that they really are your own work and that you haven't either copied or borrowed someone else's – either deliberately or by mistake (this does happen – even to established composers).

Secondly, if you have written the song with someone else, get their permission before you send it off. Mention the name of any other writers in your letter. If you don't, there could be difficulties later on. If you have used samples of somebody else's work in your recording, you should get permission for that usage from the company that owns the original recording.

It can be useful to agree who wrote what before you send your work off so that, if you are successful, you don't argue with your co-writer.

Some people worry that if they send their work away, a band or publisher could use it and make money from it without crediting or paying them. This happens rarely, but if you want to protect your work, it can help if you can prove that you are the author and when you wrote the song. One of the best and cheapest ways to do this is to take a copy of your work – on paper, on CD, or however you have set it down – and send it to yourself, in a well-sealed envelope, by registered post. Leave it unopened when it comes back to you. The dated postmark helps to prove that you had created the work by that date. This means you would be able to prove the origin of the work if necessary.

If you are certain someone has used your song without your permission, go to a lawyer first. Don't go to the record company until you have talked to someone independent.

If someone contacts you wanting to use your work, do two things. Firstly, congratulate yourself – it's a major achievement. Secondly, be very careful indeed. Most importantly, don't sign anything at all until you have taken expert advice. A general solicitor may be of use, but a specialist in media or copyright law would be better.

If someone asks you for money to publish your songs, refuse. They should be paying you, not the other way around!

The contract between you and the publisher will cover many things. The first is what you will be paid. If you are an unknown writer, this may not be very much as a publisher or record company is taking a big risk – but the more well-known you become, the better you are likely to be paid. The contract will also ask you to guarantee that your work is genuinely your own.

Don't be hurried into signing a contract. If the company really wants your work, they will want to make sure that you are happy before you sign.

If you reach the stage of signing a contract, there are a number of organisations that will help you. There are performing rights organisations all over the world which protect the work and rights of their members. There are also songwriting "guilds" in many countries, and authors of lyrics could join the Society of Authors. The Musicians Union and similar organisations world-wide will offer legal services, help, advice and protection.

This list tells you where you can find some of the main ideas in the book. It also explains some musical terms that may be unfamiliar. When a word appears in *italic* type, it is defined elsewhere in the list.

Minor   A chord which uses the notes three and seven *semitones* above its *root*. In this book, minor chords are shown with the symbol *m* after the root (22)

Notation   How music is written down (8, 9, 16, 28, 32)

Octave   The interval between a note and the next note of the same name above or below it (50)

Phrase   A short section of music, usually just a few *bars* long; the basic unit of a melody (16–17)
Pitch   How high or low a note is (18)
Poetry   (13)
Pre-chorus   A short section of a song inserted after the end of the verse and before the chorus (15)
Progression   (22–27, 33, 47)
Publishers   (31, 59–61)
Push   An accent that makes a weak beat anticipate the next strong one (40)

Record companies   (31, 59–61)
Recording   (31–33, 59)
Resolution   In terms of harmony, moving away from the *tonic* to another chord (23, 33)
Rhyme   (10, 13, 17, 22, 53)
Rhyme scheme   The order in which rhymes come in a group of lines (10, 17)
Rhythm   (8, 13, 28–30, 33, 35, 56)
Rhythm section   (31)
Root   The note on which a *chord* is based. Any note can be used as the root. Chords are usually named after their root notes (22)
Root position   The basic *voicing* of any *chord*, with the root at the bottom and the other notes over the top (22)

Sampler, samples   (58, 59, 61)
Sequencer   (32)
Seventh chord   A chord that includes the note ten semitones above its *root*. In this book, seventh chords are shown with the symbol *7* after the root (27)
Show tunes   (40)

Solo   An instrumental section inserted into a song to provide variety (55)
Stop   A point in a song where nobody plays or sings – used for dramatic effect (33)
Stresses   (11, 39)
Structure   The way a song is organised – the order of verses and choruses, for example (14, 15, 20)
Studio   (59)
Styles   (4, 6)
Substitution   Putting one chord in place of another to change the harmony (26, 47, 53)
Syncopation   An accent on a beat where it isn't expected (44)

Tempo   The speed of the beat in a song or piece of music (29)
Tension   In terms of harmony, returning to the *tonic* from another chord (23)
Texture   The sound created by a particular combination of instruments and voices (33, 44, 46, 49)
Time signature   Numbers at the beginning of written music which tell you how many *beats* there are in each *bar* (28)
Tonic   The chord on which a song is based – usually where it starts and finishes (23)
Tunes   (16–21)
12-bar blues   (22–23, 53)

Verse   The part of a song that changes each time you hear it (14, 19)
Video   (35, 51, 60)
Vocal arrangement   (49)
Voicings   How the notes of a chord are played togeher (27)

Words   (10–15, 41, 53)
Writing your ideas down   (8, 9)

... from Scratch ...

Read Music from Scratch

Can't read music? No problem!

Music is all around us, but many people think it is difficult to learn. However, once you know even the basics, it all becomes startlingly clear; a logical language where high means high and low means low.

Whether you are learning an instrument, singing or writing songs, or are just interested in finding out how music works, *Read Music from Scratch* is the book you need. It guides you through everything from clefs to chord symbols and from time-signatures to tonality. The audio CD makes written music come alive and helps you understand the language of music.

Clear, easy to use and written by experts, *Read Music from Scratch* is the ideal choice for any beginner – or for anyone who teaches beginners.

Also available . . .

BOOSEY & HAWKES

Boosey & Hawkes Music Publishers Ltd.
www.boosey.com